D0878149

Afrika, Solo

Afrika Solo
Come Good Rain
Je me souviens

edited by Ric Knowles

Playwrights Canada Press
Toronto • Canada

Afrika, Solo © Copyright 2011 Ric Knowles
Afrika, Solo: An Introduction © 2010 Ric Knowles
Afrika Solo © 1987 Djanet Sears • *Come Good Rain* © 1992 George Seremba
Je me souviens: Memories of an expatriate Anglophone, Montréalaise,
Québécoise, exiled in Canada © 2000 Lorena Gale

PLAYWRIGHTS CANADA PRESS
The Canadian Drama Publisher
215 Spadina Ave., Suite 230, Toronto, ON Canada M5T 2C7
phone 416.703.0013   fax 416.408.3402
orders@playwrightscanada.com • www.playwrightscanada.com

No part of this book, covered by the copyright herein, may be reproduced
or used in any form or by any means—graphic, electronic or mechanical—without
the prior written permission of the publisher, except for excerpts in a review,
or by a licence from Access Copyright, 1 Yonge St., Suite 800, Toronto,
ON Canada M5E 1E5 phone 416.868.1620

For professional or amateur production rights, please see the following page,
or contact the publisher for more information.

Playwrights Canada Press acknowledges the financial support of the Government
of Canada through the Canada Book Fund and the Canada Council for the Arts,
and of the Province of Ontario through the Ontario Arts Council and the
Ontario Media Development Corporation for our publishing activities.

Typesetting & Cover Design: JLArt

Library and Archives Canada Cataloguing in Publication

Afrika, solo : three AfriCanadian plays / Ric Knowles, editor.

Includes bibliographical references.
Contents: Afrika solo / Djanet Sears -- Come good rain / George Seremba --
Je me souviens / Lorena Gale.
ISBN 978-0-88754-839-0

1. Canadian drama (English)--Black Canadian authors. 2. Canadian drama
(English)--20th century. 3. Canadian drama (English)--21st century.
I. Knowles, Richard, 1950- II. Sears, Djanet. Afrika solo. III. Seremba,
George, 1958- . Come good rain. IV. Gale, Lorena. Je me souviens.

PS8307.A75 2011   C812'.54080896   C2011-900638-3

First Edition: March 2011
Printed and bound in Canada by Hignell Book Printing, Winnipeg.

Photo / Book Credits

Photo of Djanet Sears © National Post / Glenn Lowson
Photo of George Seremba © Mick Flanagan
Photo of Lorena Gale courtesy of The Estate of Lorena Gale

Afrika Solo was first published in 1990 by Sister Vision Press.

Come Good Rain was first published in 1993 by Blizzard Publishing Inc., Winnipeg, Canada. © 2005 George Seremba

Je me souviens was first published in 2001 by Talonbooks. Reprinted with permission.

To the memory of Lorena Gale, much loved and deeply missed.

Contents

Afrika, Solo: An Introduction

Ric Knowles

The three plays published in this volume participate in a genre of theatre and performance that has long been favoured by marginalized communities in Canada (albeit more for reasons of economy than any presumed natural fit): solo autobiographical auto-performance in which the author–performer (re)members, (re)invents, or (re)names her or himself through a real, remembered, or represented return to a "lost" home. Djanet Sears, citing Audre Lorde, calls this form "autobio-mythography" ("Afterword" 95). [1] In this type of work, the writer/performers use their onstage bodies as archives of cultural and individual memory, and produce, by creating a "synaesthetic relationship between subjects" onstage and off (Féral 179), startling moments of *communitas* that theorist Jill Dolan has called "utopian performatives." [2] These three plays were written and first performed by their African Canadian diasporic subjects.

Many autobiographical solo performances in this tradition map resistant and transformational continuities with a suppressed cultural past, and attempt to embody more than individualized subjectivities in a search for connection with larger diasporic communities. In his seminal 1989 book, *How Societies Remember*, Paul Connerton distinguishes between "inscribed" memory (4) and incorporating practices such as "commemorative ceremonies" (41), "bodily practices" (72), and habits transmitted from generation to generation as cultural practices. He discovers "an inertia in social structures" that is attributable to the sedimentation of memory in such embodied "performative" practices (5). In Marita Sturken's term, suggestive both for its theatrical resonances and because of its insistence on the discursive nature of such embodied practices, these are societally "prescribed" (236). Connerton's work effectively demonstrates not only the *persistence* of embodied memory, but also the ways in which such memory tends to "legitimate a present social order" (3), and from a very different angle to reinforce the most deterministic readings of Judith Butler's work on the performativity of gender (and other subjectivities)—readings that Butler herself tends to favour. [3] Arguing that gendered subjectivities are *composed* through repetition and reiteration—through "*a stylized repetition of acts*" ("Performative" 270; emphasis in original)—Butler suggests that the primary social function of performativity is to police appropriate, hegemonic behaviours, though some of her work, particularly *Gender Trouble*, holds out some hope for a more subversive repetition *with a difference*, since reproduction can never be totalizing or absolute.

I want in this introduction to connect a reading of the subversive potential of Butler's performativity within the context of a reading of Connerton by African American scholar Sandra Richards that shifts the ground somewhat to find resistant potential in the very *persistence* of embodied memory in these plays. Citing the survival of diasporic African culture in the wake of the slave trade, Richards has suggested that embodied memory, habit, and social ritual are mechanisms through which minoritized, specifically African (North) American, cultures can in fact survive in the face of repression. Indeed it was precisely this bodily transmission of cultural memory as a mechanism of cultural survival that the Canadian residential school system and the enforced removal of Native children from their families through adoption and foster parenting—the "scoops"—were designed to interrupt, operating as technologies of Canada's culturally genocidal project of assimilation. The three plays in this collection in their very different ways use embodied memory as an instrument of individual and community survival.

In the last fifteen or twenty years Canadian theatre has produced a remarkable number of autobiographical solo performances by members of minoritized groups, and a remarkable number of these performances include moments of phenomeno-logical *frisson* in which audiences connect directly and synaesthetically to the body on stage in ways that exceed the literal or semiotic communication of meaning (see States). Most of them rely on the audience's knowledge that the body they are watching bears the scars, literal and figural, of the events that the show relates; the shows, that is, refer to the writer/performer's "body as archive," in Susan Bennett's Derridean sense, for a kind of authentication, or author-ization (Bennett 45). Thus the late Lorena Gale's Black, bilingual, female, expatriate (in Canada) "Montréalaise" body seems more to performatively *present* than to theatrically *represent* the tensions that she enacts, at least as much socially as theatrically, in *Je me souviens*; Djanet Sears's anatomically diasporic body—she finds her history in "my thighs, my behind, my hair, my lips" (43)—is subject and defining object of her quest for a homeland in *Afrika Solo*; and George Seremba's *Come Good Rain* includes not only a graphic narrative of his having been shot several times and left for dead in the infamous Namanve Forest by the Ugandan military under Milton Obote, but in performance grounds that account in his visibly scarred body as archive: we as audience—or rather as *witnesses* (see Moynagh [4])—see the actual scars on his body through which the bullets passed.

In looking at these shows I am particularly interested in what I call "documem-ory," in which the performing body as archive serves up embodied traces—scars—as documents of both individual and cultural memory; I'm interested in these plays as stories about gaining, losing, choosing, changing, or earning names as social identi-fiers and cultural markers; I'm interested in them as "autobiology," performances of the social and cultural assemblage of the body becoming itself; I'm interested in the Butlerian question of the performativity of gender, race, and other social identities, particularly hybrid identities; and I'm interested in the question of the different roles that embodied cultural memory might play within the context of African Canada, where the continuities of embodied memory might be understood to replace misrepresentation—or indeed lack of representation—in dominant Canadian (and Québec) historiography.

Each of the plays published here involves some attempt to return to a home—Montreal, Africa—that is not in any real sense "there;" each involves a body that is both physically and discursively "marked" (Phelan); each involves a more or less direct statement that the autobiography being performatively constructed is not simply that of its individual author but of its historical and continuing cultural community; and each involves a moment or moments of what might be called transformative utopian performativity (Dolan).

In many ways the clearest example is Djanet Sears's *Afrika Solo*, which begins with the problem signalled in the preface to *Je me souviens* (the title of which claims participation *as* Anglo-African-Québécoise in Québécois cultural memory [5]). "It is a legacy of the African diaspora," argues Gale, "to become rooted in a land where one is always seen as 'other'" ("Going" 11). Two of the epigraphs to the first published version of *Afrika Solo* [4]—"Swing low, Sweet Chariot / Coming for to carry me home" [xiii], and "Beam me up, Scotty" [xiv]—signal its project, structure, and cultural hybridity: in spite of one passage in which the central autobiographical subject, "Janet," briefly considers plastic surgery, the show is in fact about attempting to construct or perform a coherent subjectivity by going "home," one way or another, to Africa. Home, of course, is proverbially where the heart is, but the African Canadian Caribbean protagonist of *Afrika Solo*, born in the UK, finds her heart divided: "What the hell am I doing here in my ancestral homeland, my cultural birthplace," she asks, "feeling homesick" (37)? But she does "find," or reconstruct herself, in part through performative embodiment. She recognizes in West Africa that the women's bodies resemble hers: "I began to notice that a lot of the women, well—had behinds that were just like mi—very well developed" (28). She proceeds to seeing "familiar faces" in Togo and Benin, of people who might be, or might have been, her relatives (29–30), and she is recognized there as having come back: "They always said that you would return," a West African woman tells her. "The legends say that those who were taken away by the Europeans on their big ships would return one day" (30). But when she ultimately returns to *Canada* she does so with "all my history on my back. The base of my entire culture would be forever with me. And funny thing is, it always had been. In my thighs, my behind, my hair, my lips" (43).

She does not return, however, without having undergone a performative transformation, one that recognizes her hybridized identity as "African Canadian. Not coloured, or Negro… / Maybe not even Black. African Canadian" (42). [7] Her transformation most significantly involves choice, and agency, in the construction of her social identity, one that the show seems not only to represent, but to *perform*. In the wake of a story about the so-called "discovery" and "naming" of Victoria Falls—"you know, nothing exists until a White man finds it!" (23)—the character *and actor* hitherto known as "Janet" visits the Saharan oasis town of Djanet and its nearby African rock paintings. The experience is transformational. As she writes in a postcard to her parents:

the rock paintings in Djanet are ten thousand years old. That's four hundred generations ago. Three hundred and ninety eight point two grandmothers ago. Can you imagine, people lived ten thousand years ago in Djanet? Love Janet.

She crosses out her signature and replaces in with:

D-J-A-N-E-T.

Then she breaks into rap:

> What if Jomo Kenyatta was a Robert or Paul,
> And Miriam Makeba was known as Lucille Ball.
>
> You see there's pride in a name and I can see
> Why Cassius changed his name to Muhammad Ali.
>
> A rose by any other name would smell as sweet.
> But an African called Sears sounds so offbeat.
>
> Though my family's Sears, you know what's more?
> We're related to some Sears with a department store.
>
> Though Janet rhymes with planet, what's in a name?
> I'll add a "D" to the beginning and it's Djanet again.
>
> Djanet with a "D" not Janet with a "J."
> Djanet with a "D" not Janet with a "J."
>
> I changed my being and spirit this way. (24)

In a telling final moment at the airport, the newly baptized "Djanet" (an Arabic word meaning "paradise")[8] sees her reflection in a glass door, dons her newly acquired West African Babou, and comments on something I have elsewhere called a post-colonial Lacanian mirror-stage moment of cultural identification/alienation: "you know sometimes when you look into the mirror and you sorta—catch your own I" (45; see Knowles *Shakespeare* 17). "*Her metamorphosis* […] *complete*" (45), she ends the show singing "Dat's Love" "*in her own Canadian/Caribbean/British style over the intense African rhythm*," followed by a communal African song to a Sunnu rhythm. The two accompanying performer/musicians join her, "*releasing the incantation and ending the play*" (45) that matches the "incantation" with which the show began (5), and that functions *in* performance as a utopian performative across the gap between audience and stage.

Joanne Tompkins has argued persuasively that the "metamorphosis" performed here is not, in fact, "complete," that what *Afrika Solo* represents is the *rehearsal*—"repetition *with* change ("Infinitely" 35)—of a shifting African, Guyanese, Jamaican, British, and Canadian processual subjectivity that refuses to settle into "identity" understood as something compete and finished. "The 'real' performance," Tompkins argues, "is endlessly deferred, the construction of identity is always in progress" (36). But perhaps, at least in Butler's sense, the real performance has just begun, as "Djanet" returns to Canada to (re)iterate performatively her new subjectivity on stage (in *Afrika Solo*), in life, and in labour. In a very real sense, it was with this show that Djanet Sears shifted from being an *actor* to being, not just a writer, but, individually and culturally, a *performer*. The utopian performative with which *Afrika Solo* concludes has served to mark not only Sears's own transformation-in-progress (and she has spelled her name "Djanet" only and ever since that show) but the beginnings, too, of her performative transformation of the African Canadian theatrical community, not only as a prominent playwright bringing African Canadian work into the mainstream, but also as the founding director of the AfriCanadian Theatre Festival, the editor of the two fat volumes of *Testifyin'*, the first national anthologies of African Canadian plays, the editor of the first collection of audition monologues for African Canadian actors, and the co-editor of a *Canadian Theatre Review* special issue on African Canadian Theatre.

Another playwright of African descent who has made a significant contribution as a resident of Canada, George Seremba, has produced a very different sort of auto-biographical solo performance about his relationship to his African homeland, but in the case of *Come Good Rain* the narrative is not about, but constitutes his return to Africa: it revisits, from Canada, his life in and escape from his Ugandan homeland under Idi Amin and Milton Obote.[9] Seremba is explicit about his play as the autobiography of a community, and about his responsibility to the people of Bweyogerere village, who he feels in rescuing him on December 11, 1980 from Namanve Forest, at huge risk to their own lives, had "commissioned" him to "[t]ell my story, my country's story. [...] Tell our history together (Seremba, "Playwrights" 11). The performer also presents himself as the embodiment of his ancestors in a way that is much more explicit than Sears's sharing of physical characteristics as documemory. Early in the life-narrative he provides an account of a visit to his grandmother in Rubaga, including a detour past the palace where his father tells him that his great-grandmother's father had been king of Buganda, recounting his subsequent lineage. Touching the ancient walls of the palace, George says, "My ancestors were no longer just names. They began to throb in my bones. I could touch and feel the country as though it had flesh and blood" (54). Later, left for dead in the Namanve forest, he invokes this ancestry, calling upon his ancestors by their (African) names in a kind of ritual incantation:

> You my ancestors, all of you; from Kabaka Kalema whose remains lie in Mende; Kakungulu and Mugujula, the two valiant warriors. My grandparents back in Masaka. My grandmother, Bulaliya Nakiwala, you who always danced agile as a duiker without touching a drink in your entire life. Yekoniya Zirabamuzale, you who lost your sight but never your wisdom and legendary charity. My stillborn brothers, you who never left the void, please pave my way and ease my transition. (77)

This invocation of the African names of his ancestors at the moment of his (presumed) death is a reclamation of subjectivity that the colonial system at the beginning of the show had done its best, like Canadian residential schools, to erase. At the preparatory school where he was educated, George and his fellow students were required to use their Christian names (55), to forget their "vernacular" languages (56) and, in a stereotypically racist phrase, their sense of "African time" (56). "[A]ll under thirteen. All ours, to shape and mould," (56) as the schoolmaster says, the students were taught to obliterate their African subjectivities as a foreign language was encouraged to invade their very bodies and imaginaries: "From now on you must speak English, *eat* English, sleep English, and *dream*, English" (56; emphases added).

But like *Afrika Solo, Come Good Rain* is a performance of rebirth and transformation, like *Afrika Solo* it opens with a musical incantation, and it is framed by a parallel story of rebirth from the Ugandan oral tradition, as well as by embodied ritual (53). Moreover like *Afrika Solo* it evokes community in part by involving, in its first and in most productions, an onstage musician, including, here, ceremonial drumming, in (like *Afrika Solo*) a supposed one-person show. The key moment of phenomenological *frisson* in the play and the one that produces its most powerful synaesthetic transfer of energies between the audience and the stage, is the extended account, to which I have already pointed, of the shooting of Seremba's still and visibly marked body. But the narrative itself is marked by the language of self-alienation, as if at the moment of death Seremba reverses the Lacanian mirror-stage experience of separation between the self speaking and the self represented in discourse (Lacan). As he undergoes his torture and intended murder, Seremba moves between first-person references to the self and a third-person account of what is happening to "*the* body," as bullets hit "*the* right leg," "*the* left arm," "*the* right thigh," "*the* forehead," and "*the* stomach," but another finds "*my* right hand at an angle just over *my* heart" (76; emphasis added). As one soldier aims a rocket-propelled grenade at him, "*I* stared at him in disbelief. Oh, God there goes the rest of *the* body" (76; emphases added). Once the soldiers leave, he makes detached references to "the husk that was my body" (78) and even to "the corpse" (76) that he hopes will not be lost.

Seremba's survival is recounted in the familiar literary tropes of rebirth and healing rain that are signalled by the show's title, but such tropes don't fully apply to "the body"; in fact, after the surgery that saves him, his family complains that: "they stitched our son up like a gunny bag. Only post mortem surgeons do that. *(whispers)* It's for dead bodies" (82). Indeed, it is his escape from Uganda, and Africa, that is figured as a rebirth. After a Christmas dinner at which he again pays tribute to his "African extended family" (83) and particularly his ritually named grandmother—"no amount of oppression would remove the inner dignity and proverbial wisdom of Semei Kakungulu's daughter and granddaughter of a noble King of Buganda" (84)— he begins his long journey to Kenya, then Canada, with his "new identity card. For the first time I use the name Seremba," he says (84). But the body we watch telling this story remains visibly marked by scars as the embodied traces of his ordeal— "documemory" in its most literal sense. And in spite of Marc Maufort's argument that the show "enables the protagonist to come to terms with painful memories by re-enacting them" (94), Seremba explicitly figures his performance in his "Playwright's Note" to the original publication as *not* a therapeutic journey of "getting over it" or "coming to terms," but as a struggle resistantly to *hold on* to his memories, as a "fight to *keep* some of my emotional and psychological scars—just like my country" (11–12;

emphasis added). He stresses, then, the systemic, social, and representative rather than the personal or psychological nature of his ordeal and recovery. As Modupe Olaogun argues, "*Come Good Rain* underscores the transformational potential of certain *communal* acts" ("The Need" 333; emphasis added), among them the potentially resistant, constitutive, utopian act of *communitas* that is involved in storytelling, and performance.

Like *Afrika Solo* and *Come Good Rain*, Lorena Gale's *Je me souviens* is African Canadian, explicitly autobiographical, was first performed by its autobiographical subject, and explicitly involves a "Going Home," as the playwright's prefatory note to the published text is called. But *Je me souviens* is different from Sears's and Seremba's plays in that the conflicted home it invokes is not Africa, but Montreal, the place of exile is Vancouver, and Canada is not a desti-Nation (as for Seremba), but a conflicted and evolving site of struggle, as Joanne Tompkins has demonstrated ("Remember"). This play's cultural difference is *intra*national. In fact the play's only Africa is the caricatured one of "Bunga of the Jungle" in Lorena's primary school geography class, where she is singled out as representative of Africans:

> Africans are little primitive peoples with black skin—Lorena. And tight woolly hair—Lorena. And broad flat noses, who run about the jungle naked, climbing trees for fruit, digging in the earth with crudely shaped tools for tubers and nuts, and killing elephants. (102)

Indeed, Lorena's efforts to escape the violence and racism represented by *this* "Africa," if less spectacular, are not entirely dissimilar to those of Seremba in escaping the violence of his Uganda, and they equally leave her performing body "marked" by the scars of that experience. Lorena's scars are not literal or visible in the way that Seremba's are, of course, but they inhabit her and are on display nonetheless, and some of these scars are not easily healed. The most prominent have been effected through language, which she carries inside her, in the words of post-colonial theorist Sneja Gunew, as "a kind of virus inhabiting the body" (61), the English lessons represented in *Come Good Rain* having had their full, intended, culturally genocidal effect, her "vernacular" languages completely suppressed:

> This language that I live in, this English I take shit for each time I leave home, is not my English! Each word's a link, each phrase a chain that's forged in centuries of slavery. I speak Massa's tongue. And though I've mastered the language of my subjugation, I still yearn for the authentic voices of the lost generations of my ancestry. (109)

But Lorena equally knows that "I am more than the languages I speak. Who I am is embedded in every cell of my skin" (110), and this cellular self includes and relies upon an ancestral memory that allows her to go "home," even if it's to Montreal rather than Africa, and even if it's to a Montreal that is no longer there and to a mother who has died. And the home to which she returns, fractured though it now is, constitutes for her a *community* of *embodied* memory—much of it has to do with eating, drinking, and *doing*, and much of it has to do with friends and family. As she says, "Autobiography is meaningless without context" ("Malcolm" 309).

In *Afrika Solo* Janet/Djanet discovers herself as "African Canadian" by returning to an African homeland she has never seen, adopting a new name and spirit, and performing a newly reconciled "African Canadian" self into existence. In *Come Good Rain* Seremba emerges newly alive and newly christened from apparent death and sets out for a new home with a new identity. In *Je me souviens* Lorena rejects the new, foreign name—"Loren" (107)—that is thrust upon her in her own home nation that equally rejects her (as not "pûr laine," 126) and assumes an existence as, in the words of the play's subtitle "an expatriate Anglophone Montréalaise Québecoise exiled in Canada." And only in exile in Canada, in Vancouver, where "there are no Black people" (118), is she able, through memory and performance/performativity, to find herself—invoking, perhaps ironically, the motto of Québec, "Je me souviens," which in a familiar kind of Canadian literal mistranslation can be understood to mean both "I remember," and "I remember myself." Which is exactly what she does, using the memory-journey of the play to re-member, to piece together, her disparate subjectivities.

This is not a sentimental journey. Lorena is reminded, looking at images of lynchings in the American south, accompanied by her Québécois lover who will not look with her, that "a lapse of memory could one day prove fatal" (110). Indeed, the play can be read as staging the tension between potentially oppressive, potentially fatal nationalist memory-making—the *pûr laine* version of Québec's *je me souviens* motto that in the hands of "the thousands of [Jacques] Parizeaux across Canada [...] who would seek to limit [Black or brown] participation in society"—and "the articulation of personal memory [*Je me souviens*] as political resistance" ("Going" 9). This is the same tension that Connerton, Sturken, and Butler find between the conservative, repressive role of embodied performative memory and the libratory potential of performing memory differently.

Nevertheless, or perhaps because of this, like Djanet catching her own "I," Lorena ends her play with a moment of self-recognition that I believe constitutes a powerful utopian performative. Throughout a play that is punctuated, not by theatrical blackouts, but by "whiteouts," she has reported, always in French, a recurrent dream in which, "*perdue dans une plaine de neige*" (95), in a blizzard—a whiteout—she sees and walks towards what at first is only "*un tout petit point noir*" on the horizon (115). In the penultimate scene, as she approaches that black spot in the white landscape, she comes to realize that it is a woman. As Lorena reaches out to touch her, "*Elle s'est tourné vers moi et je réalise alors qu'elle est mois./ C'est moi!*" (125). Like Djanet's celebratory realization of the plenitude of her African Canadian subjectivity in *Afrika Solo*, Lorena's recognition of "the distinct whole that is me" (126)—slyly invoking the Québecois self-recognition as a distinct society—is at once a claim and a triumph. "Memory," she concludes, "serves me" (126).

Notes

1   Lorde labelled her 1982 autobiography, *Zami: A New Spelling of my Name*, a "bio-mythography."

2   This introduction draws directly on my essay "Docu-memory, Autobiology, and the Utopian Performative in Canadian Autobiographical Solo Performance."

3   I am drawing here on Butler's essay, "Bodily Inscriptions, Performative Subversions" in *Gender Trouble* 128–41 and on her more deterministic revisiting of that essay in *Bodies that Matter*.

4   Lorena Gale also considers the audience to function "collectively," as "the witness" ("Malcolm" 311).

5   "Je me souviens"—which translates inadequately into English as "I remember," without the self-reflexive overtones of "remembering" one's self—has, since the first accession to power of the nationalist Parti Québecois, been the motto of the Quebec "nation," inscribed on every licence plate in Quebec (replacing the earlier tourist lure, "la belle province"). Gale uses it to disrupt the discourses of "pûr laine" nationalism, which exclude what then Québec premiere Jacques Parizeau, in the wake of the narrowly lost vote on Quebec sovereignty in 1995, notoriously labelled "money and the ethnic vote," including, presumably Québecois of African origin.

6   Another is from Malcolm X on African Americans' internalized self-hatred through exposure to negative Western representations of Africa (12).

7   Sears has always resisted the hyphenized "African-Canadian." Respecting that choice, I have done the same throughout this introduction.

8   According to Sears in the play (45). Joanne Tompkins provides the same translation, but says the word is Swahili ("Infinitely" 39).

9   For an account of *Come Good Rain* in the context of other plays about Idi Amin's Uganda see Oloagun, "Dramatizing."

Works Cited

Bennett, Susan. "3-D A/B." Grace and Wasserman 33–46.

Butler, Judith. *Bodies that Matter: On the Discursive Limits of "Sex."* New York: Routledge, 1993.

———. *Gender Trouble: Feminism and the Subversion of Identity.* New York: Routledge, 1990.

————. "Performative Acts and Gender Constitution: An Essay in Phenomenology and Feminist Theory." *Performing Feminisms: Feminist Critical Theory and Theatre.* Ed. Sue-Ellen Case. Baltimore: Johns Hopkins UP, 1990. 270–82.

Connerton, Paul. *How Societies Remember.* Cambridge: Cambridge UP, 1989.

Derrida, Jacques. *Archive Fever: A Freudian Impression.* Trans. Eric Prenowitz. Chicago: U of Chicago P, 1996.

Dolan, Jill. *Utopia in Performance: Finding Hope at the Theatre.* Ann Arbor: U of Michigan P, 2005.

Féral, Josette. "Performance and Theatricality: The Subject Demystified." *Modern Drama* 25.1 (1982): 170–81.

Gale, Lorena. "Going Home." *Je me souviens.* Vancouver: Talonbooks, 2001. 9–12.

————. "The Malcolm X School of Playwriting." Grace and Wasserman 309–12.

Grace, Sherrill and Jerry Wasserman, eds. *Theatre and Autobiography: Writing and Performing Lives in Theory and Practice.* Vancouver: Talonbooks, 2006.

Gunew, Sneja. *Haunted Nations: The Colonial Dimensions of Multiculturalisms.* London: Routledge, 2004.

Knowles, Ric. "Documemory, Autobiology, and the Utopian Performative in Canadian Autobiographical Solo Performance." Grace and Wasserman 49–71.

————. *Shakespeare and Canada: Essays on Production, Translation, and Adaptation.* Brussels: Lang, 2004.

Lacan, Jacques. "The Mirror Stage as Formative of the Function of the 'I.'" *Écrits: A Selection.* Trans. Alan Sheridan. New York: Norton, 1977. 1–7.

Lorde, Audrey. *Zami: A New Spelling of My Name.* (1982) Freedom, CA: Crossing Press, 1994.

Maufort, Marc. *Transgressive Itineraries: Postcolonial Hybridizations of Dramatic Realism.* Brussels: Lang, 2003.

Moynagh, Maureen. "Can I Get a Witness? Performing Community in African-Nova Scotian Theatre." *Theatre in Atlantic Canada.* Ed. Linda Burnett. Toronto: Playwrights Canada, 2010. 172–80.

Olaogun, Modupe. "Dramatizing Atrocities: Plays by Wole Soyinka, Francis Imbuga, and George Seremba Recalling the Idi Amin Era." *Modern Drama* 45.3 (2002): 331–35.

————. "The Need to Tell This Story: George Seremba's Narrative Drama, *Come Good Rain.*" *Testifyin': Comtemporary African Canadian Drama.* Vol. 1. Ed. Djanet Sears. Toronto: Playwrights Canada, 2000. 331–35.

Phelan, Peggy. *Unmarked: ThePolitics of Performance.* New York: Routledge, 1993.

Richards, Sandra. "'Snapshots of the Great Homecoming': Memorializing the Slave Trade in Ghana." Paper presented at the Cultural Memory Colloquium, Centre for Cultural Studies/Centre d'études sur la culture. University of Guelph, Guelph, ON, 10 Nov 2000.

Sears. Djanet. *Afrika Solo.* Toronto: Sister Vision, 1990.

———. "Afterword." *Afrika Solo.* Toronto: Sister Vision, 1990. 95–101.

Seremba, George. "Playwright's Note." *Come Good Rain.* Winnipeg: Blizzard, 1993. 9–11.

States, Bert. *Great Reckonings in Little Rooms: On the Phenomenology of Theater.* Berkeley: U of California P, 1985.

Sturken, Marita. "Narratives of Recovery: Repressed Memory as Cultural Memory." *Acts of Memory: Cultural Recall in the Present.* Ed. Mieke Bal, Jonathan Crewe, and Leo Spitzer. Hanover, N.H.: UP of New England, 1999. 231–48.

Tompkins, Joanne. "Infinitely Rehearsing Performance and Identity: *Afrika Solo* and *The Book of Jessica.*" *Canadian Theatre Review* 74 (1993): 35–39.

———. "Remember the Nation: Lorena Gale's *Je me souviens.*" *"Ethnic," Multicultural, and Intercultural Theatre.* Ed. Ric Knowles and Ingrid Mündel. Toronto: Playwrights Canada, 2009. 159–66.

Afrika Solo

Afrika Solo was first presented in Toronto by ASP in association with Factory Theatre and Theatre Fountainhead, officially opening the Factory Theatre Studio Café on November 12, 1987 with the following company:

JANET/DJANET	Djanet Sears
MAN ONE	Allen Booth
MAN TWO	Rudi Quammie Williams

Director	Annie Szamosi
Set and costume design	Julia Tribe
Lighting design	Leslie Wilkinson
Stage manager	Alexandra Cumberland
Associate producer	Terese Sears
Dramaturgy	Annie Szamosi

— • —

Afrika Solo was then produced at the Great Canadian Theatre Company in Ottawa, April and May 1989, with the follow company:

JANET/DJANET	Djanet Sears
MAN ONE	Allen Booth
MAN TWO	Rudi Quammie Williams

Director	Annie Szamosi
Set design	Roy Robitschek
Costume design	Esther Akinbode/Julia Tribe
Lighting design	Phillip Cassin
Stage manager	Laura Kennedy
Producer	ASP

— • —

Afrika Solo was also produced by Theatre Fountainhead as a tour for high schools in the Metropolitan Toronto Board of Education region.

Characters

JANET/DJANET A Canadian woman in her mid-twenties, British by birth, Jamaican on her mother's side, and Guyanese on her father's.

The JANET/DJANET character also plays: V.D.; HEROINE; TARZAN; MUM; DAD; MR. DINGISWAYO; MRS. NICOLAS; TOURIST; WOMAN; LIBYAN

MAN ONE Missionary. Priest. Various characters. A synthesizer player that sings and doubles on percussion as well as the accordion.

MAN TWO BENOIT's voice. DAVID. Various characters. MAN TWO is a percussionist that sings and plays everything from a djembe and congas, to the shekere, etc.

AFRIKA SOLO

THE INCANTATION

As the lights fade to black, the sound of a single drummer pounding out a Mandiani (a traditional West African rhythm) on a djembe (a traditional West African tenor drum) is heard in the distance. The drum gets louder and is soon joined by a djun-djun (a traditional West African bass drum), a cow bell, and an assortment of other percussive sounds. The Mandiani overture builds to a sensual pulse.

Singing.

ALL   Mali eh cunaka, Senegale eh cunake,
Aah ooh nana eh dia say dah.
Aah, aah, aah.
Mali eh cunaka, Senegale eh cunake.

Mali eh cunaka, Senegale eh cunake,
Aah ooh nana eh dia say dah.
Aah, aah, aah.
Mali eh cunaka, Senegale eh cunake.

Mali, Senegale, Senegale, Mali,
Mali eh cunaka, Senegale eh cunake.

THE PROLOGUE

The lights slowly fade up.

Time: Morning.

Place: BEN's room. Cotonou, Benin, West Africa.

Late morning light filters through tree-shaded windows. The room contains the suggestions of traditional Western furnishings, accentuated with striking West African decor. BEN's theme, a deep and lyrical melody, is played on a balaphone and lightly interweaves with the Mandiani overture.

DJANET places a notepad and pen on the bed.

On the floor, in the centre of the room, lie a small reinforced cardboard suitcase, a large army surplus knapsack, a Kenya bag, an ornately carved ebony walking stick, and a long strip of African fabric.

DJANET places a pile of clothing and personal effects into the centre of the strip of fabric. She ties a series of knots with the two ends of the cloth, turning it into a small shoulder bag. She places the cloth bag next to the others, indicating that her packing is complete.

DJANET picks up the notepad and pen once more, and after rereading what she has already written, she adds:

DJANET   By the time you read this letter, I will be in a plane somewhere over Senegal, on my way home. Benoit Viton Akonde. Know I love you muchly. Djanet.

DJANET tears the letter from the notepad and places it carefully on the bed. She spends several moments taking in the full consequence of her actions and then quickly collects all of the luggage.

Suddenly, without transition, the pulsing Mandiani overture is replaced by an explosion and the sound of human beatboxes. The musicians lay down a loud, infectious hip-hop rhythm with their voices.

Rapping.

I took a trip to Africa to find my root,
Let me tell ya, what I saw did not compute.

Not everyone was starving like they tell you on TV,
I never met an African who lived in a tree.

They're much more concerned with warthogs and vultures.
Than for African people, their history and cultures.

The kingdom of Mali was rich and strong.
It was four months wide and four months long.

Have you ever heard of Hausa land,
Ancient Ghana, and, and, and...

Songhai, Bornu, Abomey, look,
We need to rewrite the history book.

I'm gonna tell 'bout the journey and what happened to me,
So relax and listen and you will see.

Toronto to Tombouctou,
Nairobi to Ouagadougou.

Fasten your belt, takeoff's begun,
Seven, six, five, four, three, two…

The music explodes.

THE ACT

Time: Some day, mid-afternoon.

Place: Cotonou International Airport, Benin, West Africa.

The lights flash with an explosive charge to reveal the details of an airport.

The airport is stark, clinical, and modern, although there is something that quite clearly places us in Africa.

To one side there is an Air Afrique ticket booth and on the opposite side there is the suggestion of a waiting area. Mid-stage there is a tall stand to which a courtesy telephone is attached.

The rest of the stage is inhabited by a series of platforms of assorted shapes, sizes, and heights. They are indicative of the specific places along the journey. BEN's *room, for instance, is situated on one of the these platforms.*

DJANET *exhaustedly drops her luggage and takes a cigarette from out of one of her bags. As she is about to light the cigarette, she notices a "no smoking" sign directly in front of her. She slowly returns the cigarette to its package in her bag.*

AIRPORT ANNOUNCER ONE

(voice-over) There is an urgent call for Miss Janet Sears. Mr. Benoit Akonde paging Miss Janet Sears. Would Miss Janet Sears please pick up the courtesy telephone at the Air Afrique ticket counter.

The courtesy telephone rings.

DJANET

Shit. I guess you found my note. Shit. Why did you have to get home so early? Shit.

Okay, okay, okay, okay, okay, okay, okay, *okay… okay…*

The ringing stops.

Okay, it'll take you two hours to get here at best, by which time I hope to be cruising at a steady altitude of twenty thousand feet.

DJANET *drags her luggage to the Air Afrique ticket counter.*

To the ticket clerk.

Parlez-vous anglais?

She is relieved.

Hi, I'd like to book a seat on your three o'clock flight.... When's the next flight then...? Shit.... Oh, okay, standby on your three o'clock flight will be just fine.... Air Afrique Flight 735.... Djanet Sears.... No. S-E-A-R-S.... So how long before I can confirm a seat...? Twenty minutes.... No. No. Great.

She looks around as if trying to find something to distract her.

AIRPORT ANNOUNCER TWO

The shuttle bus to the Sheraton Hotel is now boarding.

AIRPORT ANNOUNCER THREE

Madame Camara, ton fils Juma t'attend par la bureau d'information central.

AIRPORT ANNOUNCER TWO

Air Afrique Flight 669 to Kinshasa and Kisangani is now boarding at gate number three.

In the waiting area she notices that attached to one of the seats is a small public pay television. She puts some coins in the appropriate slot and turns it on.

DJANET chuckles. She recognizes the program on the television. She hums the theme from Star Trek *loudly.*

DJANET

L'espace, la frontière finale. These are the voyages of the starship *Enterprise*, in French West Africa.

She sings to a few bars of the musical sting from The Twilight Zone.

Do do, do do.
Do do, do do.
Do do, do do!

Oh yeah. I've seen this one...

To the audience.

I've seen every *Star Trek* ever made. Yeah, yeah, this is the one where the entire crew of the *Enterprise* falls in love.

I am a TV nut; no, a TV addict. Name that theme?

She sings the theme from a popular old sci-fi TV series.

Dada dada dada dada dada dadadaah.
Daaaaaaaaaaaaaah,
Da da da da da da da da da.
Dada dada dada dada dada dadadaah,
Daaaaaaaaaaaaaaaah—

Okay, let me give you another clue then. "Danger. Danger. Warning, warning. This does not compute, this does not compute!"

You're kidding? *Lost in Space*! The adventures of the space family Robinson on their supposed journey to Alpha Centauri. Okay, how about this one?

Dada dada dada dada
Dat dah.
Way too easy.

Batman.

Oh, oh, oh, oh, oh! Now this is the mark of true TV sci-fi-it-is. Name that theme?

Ooh ooh oooh, oooh, oooh.

Oh, come on!

Ooh ooh oooh, oooh, oooh,
Ooh ooh ooh ooh oooh, oohh.

Doctor Who! The nine-hundred-year-old time lord from Gallifrey who travels through time and space in a British policeman's telephone booth. Yeah, yeah. Do you remember the Daleks? The biological robots that look like giant laser-studded thimbles. "We are the Daleks, we will exterminate you. Exterminate! Exterminate."

> *She refers to the television.*

Uh oh, Spock's in love. Look at him smile from ear to ear. That's disgusting. Can you blame him? She's stunning!

God, people on TV are just so beautiful.

And, on TV, beautiful women nearly always have gorgeously long hair.

When I was a kid, I used to put one of my father's old shirts on my head…

> *She takes her jacket off, puts it on her head, and begins caressing her newly found tresses.*

And I'd toss my gorgeously long brunette hair. Or my gorgeously long red hair. Or I'd trim my gorgeously long blond hair—just so I wouldn't get split ends.

My best friend in all the world, at the time, had long blond hair. I was living in England at the time. Sharon Vaughan-Davis—V.D. for short. We go to the same school, love the same shows on TV. This is grounds for blood sisterhood.

Well, V.D. comes over one weekend during the summer holidays.
And we were just playing in the backyard—ooh, probably
barbecuing some worms or something—when all of a sudden,
there's this great big commotion coming from my house.
Someone is screaming at the top of her lungs, "Coloured people
on television! Coloured people on television!" Oh, yeah, we were
coloured people then, we weren't Black people yet. And there were
never ever any Black people on television.

> *DJANET becomes eight years old. The airport is at once the family
> living room back home. Faint strains of the movie* Carmen
> Jones *begins to emanate from the television.*

JANET

Harry Belafonte and Dorothy Dandridge in *Carmen Jones*. It was
so fantastic! Harry Belafonte, so handsome, and Dorothy
Dandridge, so beautiful. She is the most beautiful Black woman
I've seen on TV. I mean, she looks just like Jean Harlow, Dorothy
Dandridge looks exactly like Jean Harlow—'cept she's Black.

> *Eight year old JANET imitates Dorothy Dandridge. Her
> movements are awkward and slightly out of sync with the
> music. She sings the verse to "Dat's Love," although the words
> are unintelligible, since she has no clue about the words to the
> actual song.*

> *The music swells for the big finish and JANET follows suit with
> much bravado—albeit out of key.*

That's love.
That's love.
That's love.
That's love.

> *To V.D.*

Hey V.D.! V.D.! V.D., I'm gonna be a great big movie star when
I grow up and I'm gonna marry Harry Belafonte. Janet Belafonte.
And we're gonna have six ki— What's so funny?

What's so hell funny? Oh shut up, disease-face! I know it ain't
gonna be so easy. I never said it was gonna be easy—so why don't
you just tell me something new?

> *In a thick cockney accent.*

V.D.

Janet, I am going to devote my entire life to plastic surgery. See,
I was playing doctor with Keith, at his house across the street.
And I was just giving him his physical this morning and do you
know that he has this great big—

> *She refers to her pelvic area.*

I mean, there are parts of him that definitely need to come off—
and plastic surgeons do that.

So, one: Your bum is way too big to be a movie star. But a plastic
surgeon can cut it off, and I'm going to be a plastic surgeon.
I haven't finished yet. Two: Your lips look like—well, your lips
are—way too thick. But I can cut them off. I can fix them too.
And three: Your hair. Yes, your hair…. Well it's just so…

She puts her hand in JANET's *hair.*

…so wooly. But my mum has that blond wig, yeah, remember,
yeah, that would look just great!

Silence.

Janet?

JANET runs out of the room.

Janet?

JANET   All of a sudden I don't feel so good no more. I run into my
mother's bedroom and I look at myself in the full-length mirror.

You know sometimes when you look into the mirror and sorta
catch your own eye?

She refers to the imaginary reflection in front of her.

I knew right then and there that I'd grow up to look exactly like
Dorothy Dandridge.

V.D. comes in, all of a sudden being real nice to me. She must have
figured that I was real upset, 'cause she tells me that this other
show coming on TV that has a lot of "coloured people" in it.

To V.D.

Okay, okay, slow down. So he's the king of the jungle? No, only
Doctor Dolittle can talk to all the animals! And he beats up all the
bad guys? Wow! Lots of bad guys in Africa, eh?

AIRPORT ANNOUNCER ONE

Mr. Benoit Akonde paging Miss Janet Sears. Would Miss Janet
Sears please pick up the courtesy telephone at the Air Afrique
ticket counter.

The airport reappears. DJANET *tries to ignore the announcer's
page and the ringing of the courtesy telephone.*

To the audience.

DJANET   *Tarzan.*

*Tarzan's jungle cry loudly pierces the air. The telephone stops
ringing abruptly.*

Now, I didn't expect the king of the jungle to have blond hair and blue eyes. But you soon forget about that. I mean, this guy, he really can talk to animals! Oh! Oh! Remember Cheeta the chimpanzee. Cheeta is just so intelligent—I mean Cheeta is even more intelligent than the stupid natives.

And Tarzan, he lives in this amazing tree house pad, in the middle of the jungle. It's great. It has a renovated kitchen, a bedroom with a walk-in closet, and a cane-floored living room with a beautiful view of the jungle skyline!

And Jane, Jane is an R-E-A-L, total woman.

But, like, did you ever notice, like, all the natives—I mean "coloured people," no, Black people—all the Africans, in all those Tarzan movies, are all either slaves, servants, or man-eating savage tribesmen. And they're always trying to…. Well, let me just set you up a typical scene…

> *The original melodramatic soundtrack to* Tarzan the Ape Man *is heard in the background.*

These three hunters, plus a girl—there's always a girl—are on their way to find some type of rare ivory—or something. The rare elephants that have these rare ivory tusks roam freely in an area considered to be an ancient ancestral tribal burial ground. So, the Africans get wind of this group's destination and purpose, and begin practising ancient forms of—guerilla terrorism—on the hunters. Enter Tarzan, king of the jungle.

> *Small fanfare.*

So they—Tarzan, the hunters, and the girl—after a very tiring day in the rainforest, decide to set up camp. Lo and behold, they stumble across a very quaint, but luxurious six-bedroom cottage-cum-condo—in the middle of the jungle.

Later that night, Tarzan is relaxing in his loincloth on the porch, enjoying the occasional jungle night breeze. In enters our heroine (looking as gorgeously dishevelled as ever).

Now, these women are truly, truly amazing. Always dressed to the nines—Coco Chanel safari suit, matching safari helmet, and high-heeled shoes—in the middle of the jungle.

With her hand to her forehead, panting breathlessly, she says to him, she says:

HEROINE   *(in a 1940s Hollywood starlet's voice)* Those drums… those drums, they sound so… sooo eeevil!

DJANET   She does a considerable amount of acting at this point.

Her lips begin to quiver uncontrollably.

HEROINE   Tarzan, how, how, Tarzan, can you bear to live among these… these savages?!

DJANET   And Tarzan replies, in his nice American accent:

TARZAN   *(imitating Johnny Weissmuller)* This is merely a primitive method of communication from one village to another. Get some sleep. You'll see, it will all be over by the morning.

DJANET   Next morning, drums are still going strong. Tarzan, the hunters, and the girl prepare to set off once more in search of ivory in the jungle, when, all of a sudden, the Africans begin to sing. Now this, to any well-studied *Tarzan* fan, is the cue for a tribal attack. But the Africans in every *Tarzan* movie I've seen to date, only know one song. It's true!

She sings the Tarzan movie tribal chant.

Won di
Won di eh my heh oh.

I'm serious. I know it by heart!

Won di
Won di eh my heh oh.

They don't even know another tune!

Won di
Won di eh my heh oh.

So, they start to sing the "Won di" song.

MEN   Won di
Won di eh my heh oh.

Won di
Won di eh my heh oh.

Won di
Won di eh my heh oh.

DJANET   And right on cue the Africans attack—"Geronimo!"—

MEN   *(Slapping their mouths in a Hollywood Native American battle cry)* Oo-Oo-Oo-Oo-Oo-Oh-Oh!!!

DJANET   No, no, no. Wrong movie. Oh yeah, yeah, the Africans come out of the woodwork, so to speak, throwing their spears and arrows.

The hunters are caught off guard. They've left their guns by the ammunition box, in a clearing ten metres away, and can't even convince one of their slaves to go and get them. So the hunters are forced to rush for the guns themselves, only to be cut off by a single flaming arrow which soars through the air into the ammunition box and... POW!!!

Silence.

Tarzan to the rescue.

Big fanfare.

First he saves the heroine from a fate worse than death—poison-tipped arrow in the breast. Then he flies on to one of those conveniently placed vines, hollers and beats his chest...

TARZAN's jungle cry loudly pierces the air once more.

And he swings bravely into the crowd of suddenly cowering tribesmen, who either die—instantaneously—or run shamelessly to their grass huts down the road.

The lights become very intimate as DJANET flashes back to a conversation with BEN.

Ben? Did you see *Tarzan* movies in Benin when you were growing up? Did you know that Cheeta the chimpanzee had such a crush on Johnny Weissmuller that the makeup artist had to paint Cheeta's erection black so it wouldn't be seen on camera. It's true!

The moment instantly dissolves.

To the audience.

It was lunchtime and we were all lined up in the school cafeteria. V.D., Keith, and I awaiting today's gourmet pickings.

JANET picks up an imaginary food tray.

JANET   The roast beef looked wounded. Mashed potatoes—from the powder, and cooked cauliflower.

Now, every time I see cooked cauliflower I get an overwhelming urge to vomit. So, all of a sudden like, I wasn't hungry any more. And as they slopped the cooked cauliflower onto my plate, I was trying to figure out a way to convince Keith to eat it for me. Keith would eat anything. Keith even ate the worms we barbecued in my backyard. And even Keith didn't want 'em. Then V.D. says she knows a good way of picking which one of the three of us is gonna have to eat my cooked cauliflower and she starts in with...

V.D.   Eenie, meenie, miny, moe, catch a nigger by the—

JANET   Hey, V.D.! Don't say nig—the N-word! My mum said you're not supposed to say that word. She said, it's the nastiest word you can say to any Black person... V.D. don't... V.D. I'm seri...! V.D.!!

But she just kept saying it, over and over and over again.

V.D.	Nigger, nigger, nigger, nigger, nigger, nigger, nigger, nigger, nigger.
JANET	V.D.! V.D., I'M NOT... I'M NOT...
V.D.	NIGGER, NIGGER, NIGGER, NIGGER—
JANET	V.D! V.D.! V.D.!
V.D.	Nigger, nigger, nigger, nigger, nigger, nig—
JANET	And I slap her. I slap her.

And she falls right back. And she just stares up at me, like she doesn't know who I am. And this bright red mark the shape of my hand appears on her face. Then all of a sudden she gets up and runs right to the back of the cafeteria.

Now sitting right at the back of the cafeteria is Terminal. Terminal is V.D.'s big brother. V.D.'s big brother is so big, he's the only kid in our entire school who doesn't wear a school uniform because they don't come that large. I mean, he's the kind of kid that at eleven years old goes around scalping Barbie dolls, just for fun.

So down the aisle comes Terminal V.D., and V.D. right behind him with my red hand mark on her face.

(to Terminal) Terminal, she called me nig—the N-word! My mum told us not to say that word. My mum said the N-word is the baddest—

Silence.

And I don't remember anything after that.

Try and imagine what it would feel like if someone took a Mack truck and rammed it into your face. Everyone thought I was dead. But oh no, I recover only to survive seven whole months of:

(singing) All I want for Christmas is my two front teeth.

Terminal and V.D. were transferred to another school. But I saw her once more after that. She was on my street—must have been going to Keith's house—and I was pretending not to see her, when she stops, turns right to me, on the other side of the street, and screams out:

V.D.	Why don't you just go back to where you come from!
JANET	And you know, I would have marched right across that street and slapped her again, only I couldn't exactly figure out what she was talking about. I really had no idea what she meant...

Well, my mum's from Jamaica.

Reggae music floats above her.

MAN ONE	*(singing)* Jammin'. We're jammin'.

MAN TWO	We're jammin'.
MAN ONE	We're jammin'.
JANET	But my dad, he's from Guyana.

> *A popular calypso intertwines itself with the reggae music.*

MAN TWO	*(singing)* Jean and Dinah…
JANET	And I was born in England, the same as V.D.

> *Singing.*

God save our gracious queen,
Long live our noble queen,
God save our queen.

> *All three songs are heard simultaneously.*

> *Where the hell am I from?!*

DJANET	Years later, by which time I'm the proud owner of four passports—seriously, I have a Canadian passport, a British passport, a Guyanese passport, and a Jamaican passport—I again think of V.D. Where the hell am I from?

> *DJANET picks up her luggage and once again drags it over to the Air Afrique ticket counter.*

> *To the ticket clerk.*

Hi… I'm on standby… Djanet Sears, yes… Great! One-way, please. Smoking… okay, non-smoking… Great! Just this. The rest I'll take on as hand luggage…. Thank you…. Ah, proof of citizenship. Which passport would you prefer? I've got four.

> *DJANET places four passports onto the counter.*

> *The musicians lay down a funky hip-hop beatbox.*

> *Rapping.*

If I was born in Gdansk, am I a Pole?
I may be *Solidarnoc*, but I've got soul.

I talk like a Brit from Saskatoon,
And let me tell ya, it's no damn honeymoon.

I call one day about a room for rent.
When I get to the house, he says "It just went."

And it happens all the time and it makes me wanna foam.
I just gotta get away, I'm gonna find my home.

> *DJANET clicks her heels together (à la* Wizard of Oz*).*

There's no place like home. There's no place like home. There's no place like home.

JANET	My mum and dad saw me off at the Buffalo airport.
	A slow and disjointed reggae and calypso fusion transports us to Buffalo airport.
	This is it. Here I am going back to Mother Africa. I would be retracing the steps of my ancestors, my ancestors, after four hundred years.
	My flight was cancelled. *My flight* was cancelled—until the next morning.
	I've never seen fog this bad. Me, my mum, and my dad book into a hotel across the street.
	And my mum is saying to me how much of a coincidence it is that I should be leaving home to go abroad on my own—she was exactly my age when she first left Jamaica to travel to England to study. She even tells me about her first part-time job, scrubbing the cold stone floors of the Tower of London. She nearly died of pneumonia—they treated her so badly there.
MUM	*(in a Jamaican accent)* If you ever get fed up of travelling, or you just want to come home, don't think twice about calling.
	The lights change as DJANET *flashes back to* BEN.
DJANET	You know, Ben, I've never been to the Tower of London. I lived in London for fifteen years and my mum would always refuse to take me there.
	The moment dissolves.
JANET	And my father—my father is the kind of man who only says important things. You know like:
DAD	*(in a Guyanese accent)* Get your career together before you even think of getting married.
JANET	Or…
DAD	Education. Child, you are nowhere without education.
JANET	And I guess he figured that he shouldn't send me off into the big wide world without some important lesson. Some anecdote that he could give me that would help me through the bad times and support me through the good times. And you know what he told me? He said…
DAD	Never forget to wash your underwear!
JANET	And you know, I'm still trying to decipher the true meaning, the true profundity in that statement.

At the departure gate the next morning, as I waved goodbye,
I tried to impress their image onto my mind. So I'd never forget.

To her parents.

Don't forget to write. Come and visit me when I settle down!

Bye!

JANET climbs the stairway onto the ferry.

Tunisia. Tunisia.

"A Night in Tunisia" can be heard.

All I could think about was that Dizzie Gillespie song and kissing
the African soil. Yeah, that would be my own ceremony of return.
Yeah, the first thing that I'll do is kiss the African soil.

The sea was rough that day and the ferry was three hours late.
Suddenly I see the shores of Africa. The soft rolling mountains of
Tunisia. The tip of the continent I would never leave.

*"A Night in Tunisia" cross-fades into the sound of turbulent
Mediterranean Sea waves.*

This is it! This is it! The waves are so high, though. I'm not even
really supposed to be up on deck. The bathrooms are full of
people—throwing up. Can you imagine, here it is, my first
impression of glorious Africa—

She pukes.

*JANET quickly recovers and takes a first step onto the African
continent.*

Tunisia. It wasn't just any dock. It was an African dock. Three
hours late, but here at last, here at last. Thank God Almighty, I'm
here at last.

Rapping.

The passport was stamped and the visa was checked.
But there was one more permit I had to get.

When the immigration officer started to say…

MAN TWO	The transportation office will open Monday.
JANET	I looked to the left and I looked to the right. What the hell you saying, it's Thursday night, now.

Look, I want to speak to the supervisor, mister?

MAN TWO	What you see is what you get, I am the supervisor, sister!

Friday is a holy day, on the weekends they close.
That leaves Monday morning, bright and early, six on the nose.

JANET   I was so pissed off. I was sure I would boil.
And you'll never catch me dead kissing Tunisian soil!!

> *The earth under her feet visibly changes.* JANET *finds herself walking on sand.*

The desert is like nowhere else in the world. It drew me into its womb like a lost child. Here, a few basic designs of sand, gravel, and mountains are used repeatedly and stretched to their limits, like a trial run in landscape architecture gone wrong.

Living in the Sahara is like living on another planet. Yeah, I felt as if I were on Mars.

> JANET *takes a mirror compact from out of her bag and uses it as a* Star Trek *communicating device. As she opens the compact we hear the* Star Trek *communicator beep.*

Captain's log. Star date: One nine eight four point two five. The terrain is unfamiliar, oceanic in scale; flat and unchanging for days of travel. It's amazing. Three hundred and sixty degrees of pure sand and sky.

> *The communicator beeps as she closes and replaces the compact. She takes out a small water canister.*

It's weird how you get used to having sand everywhere, all the time. In your hair, in your clothes, in your sleeping bag, in your mouth, up your nose, in your airtight flinking camera lens. But one thing you never get used to is desert water. I became a self-proclaimed water gourmet.

There was this one water I filled up with in Timiouahne. So this water, okay? It's grey. I'm serious. The more I drink of this water, the thirstier I get. It has the consistency of liquefied Jell-O and tastes like Maalox. I even tried mixing it with Tang or lemonade. Can you imagine lemon-flavoured Pepto-Bismol?

In the driest parts of the Sahara, I was limited to two litres of water a day. To drink and bathe in. I got it down to an art. I can wash my entire body in one cup of water.

> JANET *pours water from the canister into a small bowl.*

But on those days when I did fill up with water, luxury. I would fill a small wash basin practically to its brim and find a secluded spot behind some nearby sand dune. The sun would have just left the sky and the moon would have already taken its place. I'd take off all my clothes—feel the warm air against my skin. The stars flickering in the immense sky. And I'd slowly wash.

It was a ritual, I guess.

She performs a washing ritual.

I'd wash the sand from out of my eyes, from out of my ears, from off my skin. I'd wash the sand from out of my mouth and from between my toes. But I'd never be able to wash the African sand from out of my soul.

Singing.

Twinkle, twinkle, little star,
How I wonder what you are.
Up above the world so high,
Like a diamond in the sky.
Though I know not what you are,
Twinkle, twinkle, little...

Stars like diamonds,
Alone under the crowded sky,
Makes you wonder why.
What is in this human heart,
That longs for love and that reaches for the...

Stars like diamonds.
I long for someone to hold me tight,
And share this wondrous sight.
Arms wide open, let me in.
Then I'll outshine these bright pulsating...

Stars like diamonds.
Isolated, far from home,
How much longer will I roam.
I seek a place where I fit in,
And I'll search until I find it,
I'll look up around and behind it.
I'll know if when I get there,
'Cause I'll sleep within your arms under the stars.

One day, after weeks of sand or gravel plains, on the horizon appeared one of the most beautiful oases I ever saw. Like in a mirage, a mountain of green appeared from out of nowhere.

The oasis town of Djanet. D-J-A-N-E-T. It means "paradise" in Arabic. The water in Djanet gushed out of the earth, out of her core, clear and abundant. It tasted so sweet.

Djanet is also the gateway to the secret of the Tassili plateau. The ten-thousand-year-old Saharan rock paintings. Two of the more famous paintings depict beings that wear helmets over their heads and space suits. In one of the paintings, the one called the

Martian, the being has only one eye. In fact experts have actually speculated on visitations from outer space.

Have you noticed that if an anthropologist goes out and studies an ancient "third world" culture, and he finds knowledge or traditions way in advance of his own, he always ends up speculating on visitations from outer space. I've noticed that.

Anyhow, to be able to see these rock paintings, one has to get written permission from the chief tourist officer in Djanet. You see, the department does not allow unphysically fit or overweight visitors to climb the four thousand metre volcanic mountain route to the paintings. (It seems that past experiences with unfit visitors have resulted in emergency rescues by helicopter for cases of heart attack and physical exhaustion.)

But I line up outside Mr. Dingiswayo's office door anyhow.

She walks to the end of an imaginary queue.

Oh, shit! He's asking that woman in front of me to stand aside, and she's not even that fat. Shit, he's never going to let me go now.

Confidence, Janet. Confidence!

I hand him my form and he looks up at me. (Probably assessing the bulk.)

In a deep North African accent.

DINGISWAYO   Where do you come from?

JANET   Canada, sir.

DINGISWAYO   Oh Canada, eh?

JANET   (He's probably never seen a Black North American woman in his life.)

But my ancestors are from Africa. We've been away for over four hundred years!

DINGISWAYO   Ah, like Kunta Kinte, eh? Here, enjoy your journey!

JANET   The four-hour climb nearly killed me. But I made it.

JANET takes out a camera and begins to take photographs.

The paintings are spectacular. Fifty or sixty major works. They range from ochre and charcoal impressions of elephants, antelope, lions, and wild animals, to detailed etchings of people with herds and herds of cattle—in the middle of the desert. I had to keep looking around, just to remind myself of where I was. And these were African people.

You see, over forty-five hundred years ago, when the green Sahara began turning to sand, these people migrated. Some southward where they developed a kingdom called Great Zimbabwe which stretched from the Zambezi to the Limpopo rivers. And some to the northeast, to Nubia and Egypt, where they developed one of the greatest and most powerful civilizations in antiquity.

The lights become drastically brighter.

Then all of a sudden. There I am, in Mrs. Nicholas's class—there I am, seven years old, the only Black kid in my class.

In a high-pitched upper-class British accent.

NICHOLAS   I am disgusted at the way those coloured people are reacting to the death of Martin Luther King. They are rioting in the streets, looting innocent merchants, even killing people. We did not rampage nor kill people when John F. Kennedy died, did we? I am not surprised that the American police are locking them up behind bars. Civilized human beings do not act that way.

JANET   And she's looking right at me. Mrs. Nicholas. And I don't know what to say. All I can think is—

Her hand shoots up into the air.

Miss, I have to pee.

DJANET flashes back to BEN.

DJANET   Civilized human beings, eh? What is it you said, Ben? "Civilization is merely the art of building cities."

The moment dissolves.

"Baa Baa Black Sheep" and "Mary Had a Little Lamb" are heard being played very simply in the background.

Once upon a time, a European traveller, while in southern-most Africa doing some geological research (as well as some missionary work on the side), became very good friends with some Zulu people. One day, one of the Zulu men told the European of an amazing site, and he and a few of his Zulu friends took the European traveller to see this awe-inspiring vision.

When they arrived the European was breath-taken.

"What is it called?" the European cried.

"Called?" replied the Zulu. "It is called the great waterfall."

"The great waterfall, eh," repeated the European.

So right then and there the European renamed and christened the great wonder himself. He christened it Victoria, after his great queen. And from that day forward, generation after generation have read in the great history books: Victoria Falls, discovered by—David Livingston.

The nursery rhyme stops abruptly.

You know, nothing exists until a White man finds it!

DJANET flashes back to BEN.

Remember the French map in the palace, Ben. It gave away the Frenchman's true first impressions of Benin and its people. They called the country "Le Royaume de Judas," The Kingdom of Judas.

The moment dissolves.

Back in the airport, DJANET takes a notepad and pen out of one of her bags and begins to write.

JANET   Dear Ben… I know that you—

She rips the paper out, throws it away, and begins to write again.

Dear Ben… Je sais que—je sais que—

She rips this one out too and begins once more.

Dear Ben…

This time she crosses his name out and replaces it with:

Dear Mum and Dad…

JANET is immediately transported back to the Sahara. She continues writing.

The rock paintings in Djanet are ten thousand years old. That's four hundred generations ago. Three hundred and ninety-eight point two grandmothers ago. Can you imagine, people lived ten thousand years ago in Djanet? Love Janet.

She crosses out her signature and replaces it with:

D-J-A-N-E-T.

Rapping.

DJANET   What if Jomo Kenyatta was a Robert or Paul,
And Miriam Makeba was known as Lucille Ball.

You see there's pride in a name and I can see
Why Cassius changed his name to Muhammad Ali.

A rose by any other name would smell as sweet.
But an African called Sears sounds so offbeat.

Though my family's Sears, you know what's more?
We're related to some Sears with a department store.

Though Janet rhymes with planet, what's in a name?
I'll add a "D" to the beginning and it's Djanet again.

Djanet with a "D" not Janet with a "J."
Djanet with a "D" not Janet with a "J."

I changed my being and spirit this way.

AIRPORT ANNOUNCER ONE

Mr. Benoit Akonde paging Miss Janet Sears. Would Miss Janet
Sears please pick up the courtesy telephone at the Air Afrique
ticket counter.

> DJANET *shouts as if trying to kill the incessant ringing of the
> courtesy telephone.*

DJANET   *Hot!*

> *The ringing stops.*

It was so hot. Nearly one hundred and twenty degrees Fahrenheit
in the shade. It was so hot here all I could think about was how
cold it was that first winter in Canada.

What a culture shock—London, England, to Saskatoon,
Saskatchewan. I was fifteen, the height of my pubertal social life,
and the only Black kid in my entire school now. The other kids
would even come up to me and ask to touch my hair and stuff.

And look, I was used to the cold. London, England, isn't exactly
the Montego Bay of Europe, you know. But this was ridiculous.
I nearly freaked right flinking out the first time the hairs in my
nose froze. And snow…

> *Singing in a broad calypso style.*

Saskaberia, Saskatchewan.
The true north flinking pole.
Frost biting ya fingers,
Chill eating ya skin,
Snow up in ya asshole,
The air so cold it sting.
The Earth was made to live on
I know I read it in a book,
But I just can't go on living
Like a palm tree in a toque.

Now everybody sing…

And here I was only days away from Tombouctou, where in 1324
one of the world's first universities was built. Here I was only days
away from Tombouctou, thinking about snow. Dreaming about

a nice cool, freezing-cold Blue, or Molson Golden. And thank God I'm in Mali now, because you can't get beer in Algeria.

See, Algeria is a Muslim country. You know, the women are covered from head to toe in black—from head to toe—in the middle of the desert.

Okay, I've got a good one for you. If Buckwheat became a Muslim, what would he be called.

Kareem of Wheat! Okay… okay… okay…

DJANET flashes back to BEN.

I couldn't believe my ears. Here we were in the fetish market, in the vodun section, and I ask you about the different Yoruba gods and what they stand for, and you say: "I don't know. I don't know, I'm Catholic." Catholic!

The moment dissolves.

Catholic. Even my short-lived excursion into Christianity taught me that had I not been lucky enough to be the descendant of a slave, I would be among the millions of heathenistic savages basically doomed for hell barring a visit from one of the missionaries they were sending down to the "dark continent" to save us sinners from an eternity of darkness. Oh, Ben!

The moment dissolves.

MISSIONARY   We come as members of a superior race to spiritually elevate the more degraded parts of humanity.

Singing.

ALL   Onward Christian soldiers
Into heathen lands.
Prayer book in your pockets,
Rifles in your hands.
Take the happy tidings
Where trade can be done,
Spread the peaceful gospel
With the Gatling gun.

"Rock of Ages" is sung in Swahili and can be heard in the background.

DJANET puts her hammock together.

DJANET   Just like Kenya, I mean, I was in Kenya, living with the Turkana—you know, the people who stretch their necks with layers upon layers of glass beads?

Well, I'd just hitched my tent to the back of Mr. David Malequa's grass hut. David and I got along real well. See, I was almost fluent in Swahili by now and David Malequa knew almost seventeen words in English.

This may just be it. This may just be what I've been looking for.

Now this teeny tiny village of about, oh, some seventy people or so, seemed to be able to support two fully constructed brick churches. One's Baptist and the other one's Catholic.

One afternoon, David Malequa, my Turkana host, tells me that a priest from the land where the big Catholic chief lives is coming here to Turkana, to give Mass.

When I get to the church, aside from finding the entire village there—it seems that the entire village plays the role of congregation for both churches—I also notice, that all the women are wearing rosary beads at the bottom of their already impressive collection of glass beads. This is my first clue to why Catholicism is still thriving in Turkana land!

Now the visiting priest isn't from Rome at all, this guy's from Barcelona. But, you see, I don't realize until five minutes into the Mass that it's actually English he's speaking. And, listen to this, David, the guy who's hut I'm hitching my tent to, is standing next to the priest, translating the priest's English into Swahili. Please recall that David only knows seventeen words in English. And even I can't understand what the priest is saying.

Oh yeah, I forgot one thing. David is Muslim.

The Swahili hymn stops abruptly.

PRIEST   Hallelujah!

                DAVID translates the English into Swahili.

DAVID   *Yesu ni M'luya!*

                DJANET translates DAVID's interpretation back into English.

DJANET   Jesus was a member of the Luya tribe.

PRIEST   Jesus Christ was a Jew!

DAVID   *Hata Yesu allitumia schoo!*

DJANET   Even Jesus went to the toilet.

                Holy…. Leave North America and come to live in a teeny tiny village with two churches?

                She quickly dismantles the hammock.

When I was younger, all this darkness was being heaped upon me. "It will be a 'black day' when the lord descends to judge us all if every man, woman, and child has not heard the word of Jesus Christ our saviour." Black day, eh? Well, if it's going to be a black day, I suspect that I will do very well!

Back in the airport, DJANET *pulls out a crossword puzzle.*

Okay, nine letters that mean "a longing for familiar circumstances that are now remote"? My love life. Doesn't fit anyway. Oh, oh, nostalgic. Now, seven letters that mean "ancestor worshipper," beginning with "C"? Cannibal? Eating someone could be a form of worship. Maybe not. Ancestor worshipper, beginning with "C"?

No, no, no, no, no. Not nostalgic, nostalgia. So seven letters that mean "ancestor worshipper," beginning with the letter "A," is animist.

Dogon drumming begins.

The Dogons are animists. They worship nature and the spirits of their ancestors. The neat thing about worshipping your ancestors is that you live your life knowing you too will become an ancestor one day. Sure, I could learn to get into that.

Putting away her crossword puzzle she makes her way towards what becomes the Dogon village.

The Dogons live in areas that are difficult to access. That's why neither the Muslims nor the Christians have managed to convert them from their "savage ways."

As you look down onto the Dogon village from the mountaintop, you can see a collection of houses and granaries all crowded together, flat roofs of clay alternating with cone-shaped roofs of straw.

Some of the Dogons would point or stare, others would actually come up to me and say something that sounded like "Dogoni, Dogoni?" As if to say, you're one of us, aren't you? You're one of us.

But even with a translator there, I felt an enormous communication gap between myself and these people. These people I wanted to know.

I decided that I should be moving on. I had picked up a few words in Dogon by now. I woke up early that morning and I made my way along the narrow streets of light and shade, to a large rock in an open area. This I figured could be considered somewhat the centre of town. I sat down on this rock which divided two pathways and proceeded to say hello in Dogon to every man, woman, or child that passed me by. I stopped everyone.

Ouh sayawa?

MAN ONE   *Ouh man a sayawa.*

DJANET   *Sayawa?*

MAN ONE   *Sayawa.*

MAN TWO   *Ouh sayawa?*

DJANET   *Ouh man a sayawa.*

MAN TWO   *Sayawa?*

DJANET   *Sayawa.*

It felt so good, just saying "Hello, how are you?" "*Sayawa.*" *Sayawa.…* Geez. I wonder if that's where, "Say what?" comes from?

AIRPORT ANNOUNCER ONE

Mr. Benoit Akonde paging Miss Janet Sears. Would Miss Janet Sears please pick up the courtesy telephone at the Air Afrique ticket counter.

The courtesy telephone rings.

DJANET *takes a knife and a large ripe mango from out of her bag. She cuts the fruit open and eats it succulently, as West African highlife music surrounds her.*

DJANET

In most of rural Africa, the marketplace is the centre of the world. Like Wall Street. A barrage of sound, colour, smells, and things I'd never seen before. Like the Eaton Centre, the Saturday before Christmas.*

I must have hit every marketplace from Tombouctou to Nairobi. It's the only real place you can actually just sit and people-watch. And the people! Most of the men in West Africa wear long regal gowns and tall embroidered hats. And the women.… Ahh, the women.

I began to notice that a lot of the women, well—had behinds that were just like mi—very well developed. Yeah, they had these voluptuously developed hips. And their lips, their lips were sensuous and full. And their hair—oh, you should have seen the coifs and the many intricate styles of head wraps. God, this is beautiful! The women adorn themselves with these stunning fabrics and jewellery.

---

*   The name "Eaton Centre" can be substituted for the name of the most popular shopping centre in the region.

*She puts the mango down and picks up one of the lengths of
West African fabric that adorn the stage.*

Isn't this just gorgeous! I bought seventeen of these in one
marketplace.

*The West African highlife cross-fades into a Masai rhythm.
DJANET slowly wraps the material around her body, folding and
pleating the material into a traditional West African style.*

I lived with the Masai for three months. They're amazing people.
They're basically a nomadic people who take care of their many
herds of cattle. You know, the more cattle you have, the more
status you acquire. Well, their concept of beauty is completely
different. The men and women wrap themselves in layers and
layers of loose material. The women wear pounds of beautifully
beaded jewellery. In fact, the women stretch their earlobes and the
closer her earlobe is to her shoulder the more beautiful she is.

Like I mean, Dorothy Dandridge would not have made it here.

I spoke fluent Swahili at the time as well as a few words in Maa,
the Masai language, and I had the privilege of playing tour guide
from time to time for the tourists who came down to the Masai's
"encang," their small encampment. And the questions some
tourists would ask. One woman, after taking a tour of the Masai
village, actually had the gall to say…

TOURIST *(in a broad White southern US accent)* Is the Masai's lack of
conventional clothing in any way linked to some type of native
sexual rite?

DJANET On the other hand, after the tourists had left, the Masai would
hold major dialectic discussions on why Westerners wear clothes
that hold in their farts!

*Wearing the West African wrap in some way transforms her.
The metamorphosis begins. "Dat's Love," the song from*
Carmen Jones *is reprieved with subtle West African rhythmic
adjustments.*

That's love.
That's love.
That's love.
That's love.

It was really quite eerie, you know. In some parts of Togo and
Benin, on the West African coast, I began to see familiar faces.
I began to recognize people. There was this one man, selling
souvenirs at the grand market in Lomé, that was the spitting

image of my uncle Jim. I must have used up about two roles of film just taking pictures of him to show my dad.

Pointing to some passersby.

Auntie Norma!

Oh my God, Uncle Vibert.

Ratid hole, there's Mr. Ackee, the man who owns the Jamaican patty shop up on Eglinton.*

And by the way, Eddie Murphy's double's name is Senou Batande, and he lives at seventy-nine Magamate St., Ouidah, The Republic of Benin. I'm serious!

At the Grand Marché, the grand marketplace here in Cotonou, the capital of Benin, a woman selling mangoes, passion fruit, bananas, and an assortment of birth control pills asked me if I was an "Américain noire," a Black American. So I explain to her that I live in Canada. Then she said something that surprised me.

WOMAN   *(in a broad West African accent)* So you did come back.

DJANET   Pardon me?

WOMAN   They always said that you would return. The legends say that those who were taken away by the Europeans on their big ships would return one day.

                Silence.

DJANET   At that moment I knew I'd arrived. Here at last was the gold carpet laid out to greet me. It all felt so familiar, yet, at the same time, so unfamiliar. I mean, I was home, but I didn't know anyone or anything here. Somewhere in the last four hundred years I'd lost a major connection with this place.

                I should have stayed in Benin right then and there, but I'd booked my passage to Nigeria already—I had my bus ticket in my pocket. I wanted to leave her some memento of my passing. I had a CityTV T-shirt and a pin of the Canadian flag—the T-shirt was dirty, so I gave her the pin. I'll never forget her.

                The airport reappears.

AIRPORT ANNOUNCER ONE
                Mr. Benoit Akonde paging Miss Janet Sears. Would Miss Janet Sears please pick up the courtesy telephone at the Air Afrique ticket counter.

---

* "On Eglinton" may be substituted for any well-known area or street name populated by Caribbean people or Caribbean stores (i.e., "in Brooklyn").

The courtesy telephone rings. This time DJANET *approaches it.*

DJANET   Oh Ben.

The ringing stops.

One day I came across a book in the library. I'm a procrastinator. I had an essay due the next day on teenage skin problems for my health class, and I was looking in the index for a book on blackheads and acne. There was nothing under blackheads, but I came across this one book called *Black People Black Kingdoms*. I immediately vetoed checking dermatitis under the subject listings and jotted down the call number for this *Black Kingdoms* book.

This book was the first truly amazing book I'd ever read—not counting *The Jackson Five Story*. I read about the many West African kingdoms, their kings and queens, princes and princesses. Nzingha, the renowned warrior queen in the Kingdom of Ndongo. Mansa Musa, emperor of the great Kingdom of Mali. Yaa Asantewaa, queen mother of the Ashanti state of Ejisu.

It had glorious pictures of palaces and structures of worship. I never learned any of this in school. There was even a chapter that stated that there is scientific basis for the ancient potions of African witch doctors that Western medicine has only begun to investigate.

I began this fantasy about being a long-lost African princess. I could be royalty and not even know it.

DJANET flashes back to BEN.

Benoit Viton Akonde, when you told me that your great-grandfather was the last king of Abomey, I nearly croaked. (My sisters will die when they hear this one.)

The moment dissolves.

So, I'm on my way to Lagos, when…

Rapping.

At the border to Nigeria
A scene of mass hysteria

Hoards of people can't get through
No one knows just what to do.

Excuse me, sir, open up the gate,
I must be in Lagos at eight.

MAN TWO   Turn around, please, you must go back
Or I'll start acting like a maniac

	This border is shut for several days Unforseen technical delays.
DJANET	Look, I don't want to misconstrue So I ask them to tell me why can't I get through.
MAN ONE	Our currency is devaluating Contraband, black market is escalating.
MAN TWO	Psychic quasi rent, fiscal reconciliation Zero base market force needs rectification.
DJANET	I didn't understand what he was saying to me You see I failed economics at university.
	Hey, the poetry's nice, sir, but what are you saying Am I going to Nigeria or am I staying?
MAN TWO	The borders are closed to change the colour of our money, Our currency's the naira—honey.
DJANET	The plates are now in England to be printed, I learn.
MAN ONE	The borders are closed till they return.
DJANET	Six days later things get weird.
BOTH MEN	Two barrels of new naira have disappeared!
DJANET	Two barrels of new naira have disappeared!

Do do, do do.
Do do, do do.
Do do, do do!

So I'm stuck in Benin. And amongst other things, I've contracted a severe case of the "I am sick of living in a tent" blues. I mean, here I was camped out behind the kitchen of a two-star hotel. But it was conveniently right across the street from the Benin Sheraton Hotel—which had a grand five-star rating.

One of the interesting things about the Benin Sheraton was that once inside, I may as well have been sitting in the Four Seasons— you know, at Avenue Road in Yorkville.* It was plush. Filled with plush carpet, plush furniture, even the food was plush.

The stand to which the courtesy telephone is attached revolves to reveal a bar. Piano lounge music can be heard in the background.

---

* The name and location of this hotel may be substituted with the name and location of the most exclusive hotel in the region.

So here I am standing at the bar drinking my Grand Marnier and orange juice—listen. I have slept in a tent every night for the last seven months, the least I can do is treat myself.

She drinks.

Then the waiter tells me that a certain gentleman would like to buy me another round. Well, I have only seen this kind of thing happen in the movies.

The waiter points to the gentleman in question.

She glances in his direction.

Oh my God, he's a knockout. Tall, dark, very dark, and very handsome. Our eyes meet across the crowded room.

After about an hour or so of exchanged glances I find myself in complete lust with this man. Oh…. Oh no—he's leaving. Oh…. Oh God—no—he's coming this way. Oh. He's coming over to the bar. Oh my Go…

DJANET *smiles widely.*

Hello! Oh, of course, please join me.

(He's a Libyan expatriate. He's even more beautiful up close. What slender hands. What a charming smile. What a—oh shut up, Djanet, you're beginning to sound carnivorous.)

In a lush, sexy Libyan accent.

LIBYAN	You are on your way to Nigeria, are you not?
DJANET	(Oh God, he's psychic too!)
	Yes, but the borders are closed, they say—
LIBYAN	I know, I saw you at the border last week. I am also stranded…
DJANET	(What luck, he's stranded too.)
LIBYAN	I was wondering, would you be interested—in buying some freshly printed Nigerian naira?
	Pause.
DJANET	You mean… the stuff that they've just had printed in England?
	The LIBYAN *smiles widely.*
LIBYAN	Hmm hhmn.
DJANET	You mean… the stuff that they haven't even distributed yet?
LIBYAN	Hmm hhmn.

DJANET	At which point a beautiful Black lady with long flowing braids taps him on the shoulder and whispers in his ear. He smiles. He then tells me that he has to leave and cites important business.
LIBYAN	But here is my room and telephone number, should you need my assistance.
DJANET	They leave the bar, arm in arm.

What an asshole. Why do I always fall for assholes. I swear he will be the last one.

The bar disappears.

DJANET mutters an array of sorrys and excuse me's as she attempts to get to an empty seat in the middle of an imaginary row of already seated people.

So imagine. Here I am in Benin, a tiny little country in West Africa, at an outdoor cinema, watching:

She sits.

Maurice Chevalier, Leslie Caron, and Louis Jourdan in *Gigi*.

In Maurice Chevalier singing voice, while accompanying himself on a French accordion.

MAN ONE	Thank heaven for liddle girls...
DJANET	This is weird, this is really weird!

So it starts to pour and everyone rushes to the lobby but me— look, I've always wanted to see the end of *Gigi*.

Then I hear this voice:

MAN ONE	Thank heaven for liddle girls...

In a deep French/West African accent.

MAN TWO	It's nice and dry under here.
DJANET	(Oh no, another black-market Romeo.)

No, thank you very much, that's very kind of you.

MAN ONE	Thank heaven for liddle girls...
MAN TWO	Are you with the Peace Corps?
DJANET	No, I'm afraid not.
MAN TWO	You must be with CUSO then?
DJANET	(I knew it. I knew it. I can now spot an asshole within thirty metres of me.)

No, I'm not with CUSO. I'm just a traveller.

MAN TWO	Ah huh!

MAN ONE	Thank heaven for liddle girls…
MAN TWO	What do you think of the movie?
DJANET	What is this, *Entertainment Tonight*?
MAN ONE	Thank heaven for liddle girls…
	Well, it beats *Tarzan*.

> *Pause.*

DJANET	Pardon me?
MAN TWO	Last week they showed *Tarzan. Ivory in the Jungle.*
DJANET	You're kidding!
MAN TWO	I am quite serious.
DJANET	That's the one where the two hunters and the girl are trying to find some type of rare ivory or something and the rare elephants that have these rare ivory tusks roam freely in an area considered to be an ancient…

> *Overlapping.*

MAN TWO	…ancient ancestral tribal burial ground. I am Benoit Viton Akonde. How do you do?
DJANET	You know, I don't think I've ever seen the end of *Gigi*.
MAN ONE	THANK HEAVEN FOR LIDDLE GIRLS!

> *DJANET re-enters BEN's room. She reclines on the bed.*
>
> *To BEN.*

DJANET	Benoit Viton Akonde, twenty-eight, born in Benin, recently returned from France where you'd spent the past ten years. I liked your style: a sort of Western/African. Fitted jeans under a traditional dashiki. Cute, real cute, and real…

> *She sits up.*

When you took me to the palace. How in the hell did you get a key to the palace? And you say, quite nonchalantly, that your great-grandfather was the last king of Abomey. So you're my African prince, huh?

At the palace, I get my own personal tour of the many buildings encircled by the ornately carved palace wall. All the Black history I'd ever learned in school suggested that Black history began with slavery. Well I was now standing in a place that suggested otherwise.

The throne room was amazing. Each king had his own throne designed to his own particular taste. And each had his own flag which would symbolize what he wished for his people. The rooms were filled with ancient artifacts, carvings, utensils, and musical instruments, hundreds of years old.

She walks toward BEN. *The sound of Dahomian drums hover in the background.*

I can still see the large building that was the holding area for prisoners and slaves who were to be sold off to the Europeans. I'd never really made the connection that Africans had anything to do with the slave trade. But it wasn't just that. I know that those Africans who did aid in the slave trade were mainly protecting themselves. I knew that if they didn't raid other nations and sell those peoples to the Europeans, they themselves would be at risk of becoming slaves. So it wasn't just that.

Haitian drumming replaces the Dahomian drums, creating an ominous tension.

Remember that picture? The one that depicted the many ways in which the slaves were piled up, one atop the other in the slave ships which were to cross the Atlantic Ocean to the colonies.

I had seen pictures like this in history books. But it wasn't just that.

Singing very slowly.

Swing low, sweet chariot.

Four hundred years ago, I, the descendant of slaves, may have stood here myself. And you, the descendant of African kings, standing right behind me, would have been selling me to the White man to save your own life. This might actually be where my journey began four hundred years ago. And I could see how we were packed like sardines. Fifteen million human beings transported like canned fish, for months on end, thousands of miles from home.

She sings.

Coming for to carry me home.

Then you put your hands on my shoulders. And we stood there, glued to time for what seemed to be hours.

Drumming ends.

Ben, I wasn't angry at you when we left the palace that day, you know. Listen, I say these words whenever I feel like I'm getting involved in something dangerous. "Look, I'm really not interested in seeing anyone on an intimate basis right now. I relish my freedom and get real demanding in relationships. I have a lot of things to do with my life and I really don't want to get tied down."

BEN   I see. So what time should I pick you up tomorrow then?

             Slight pause.

DJANET   Ah…. Ten's just fine with me.

             Shit!

             I was so embarrassed that day at the post office. I was just so excited to get a parcel from my family. I ripped the package open right then and there and several pairs of women's underwear in assorted pastel shades fell like autumn leaves to the ground for everyone to see. And you just picked up my panties and stuffed them in your jacket pocket. Oh. God!

             I didn't eat lunch that day. Too busy. Too busy crying over the packet of Dunhill cigarettes my sister Rosie sent me. Laughing at the CityTV T-shirt my sister Terese sent me. The stuffed toy rabbit my baby sister Celia gave me, and the photos of all of them my parents sent me.

             What the hell am I doing here in my ancestral homeland, my cultural birthplace, feeling homesick.

             And I ask you why you came back to Benin.

BEN   *Les Français, ils sont racists.*

DJANET   Ben, you know you even have a way of making the word racist sound sexy.

BEN   In France I am a second-class citizen. I get angry just thinking about it. After having spent most of my adult life in France, I felt that I now needed the comfort—is that the right word?— the support of my own family and my own culture.

DJANET   You knew what your culture was.

             Family, you said, is a strange phenomenon. No matter what happens, they…

             Overlapping.

BEN   …they are always your family. It is one of the strongest kinds of bonds we human beings ever know.

             It is late at night. DJANET *and* BEN *lay in bed.*

             Djanet?

DJANET   Yes, Ben.

BEN   Are you sleeping?

DJANET	No, sweetheart, I'm not sleeping.
BEN	Teach me that song again.
	Singing.
DJANET	We shall overcome.
BEN	We shall overcome.
DJANET & BEN	We shall overcome some day.
DJANET	Oh, deep in my heart,
BEN	Oh, deep in my heart,
DJANET	I do believe,
BEN	I do believe,
DJANET	That we shall overcome some day.
BEN	Oh, deep…
DJANET & BEN	…In my heart, I do believe, That we shall overcome some day.
BEN	I like that song. Teach it to me again.

All traces of BEN dissolve.

The airport reappears.

AIRPORT ANNOUNCER ONE

Air Afrique Flight 735 to Paris, London, New York, and Buffalo, is now boarding. Will all passengers kindly make their way to gate number nine.

DJANET   That's me. I'd better hurry.

DJANET pulls out a bottle of Grand Marnier.

It's not that I'm afraid of flying, it's just that I like to be real relaxed when that thing takes off. I prefer to have my two feet planted firmly on the ground at all times. But since I have no choice in the matter, I'd rather my brains were flying too.

Here's to taking the train—

She drinks from the bottle.

—or walking!

She drinks again.

In the last year, I have walked so far, that if…

Let me tell you one more story. It's about…. Well you'll see what it's about.

At Epulu Station, in Zaire, I hire two rangers to guide me twenty-eight kilometres into the Ituri Rainforest—better known as the jungle, to meet the BaMbuti people—better known as the pygmies.

BaMbuti music begins. A sound collage of voice and mbira (Cental African thump piano).

Now, the jungle is out of this world, because of the thick canopy of trees and flora, it's always either twilight or pitch black. And it stinks in the jungle. Seriously, everything is either dying, dead, or coming back to life. And when you walk in the jungle, you sink about ten centimetres down into the ground with each step, into layer after layer of this dying, dead, or coming back to life stuff.

We walk for nine hours to get to this particular BaMbuti settlement. Nine full hours. But when we finally arrive at the encampment the chief comes out to greet us.

Now, I've never stood face to face with a real live pygmy before and the first thing that you notice about him, is that he's really—short.

The clan must have had a good day's hunting because he immediately invites us in to eat with them. The choice of entree: roast monkey or—dik-dik.

Now, I would have selected the monkey, because I pride myself on being able to question cultural taboos. But when we entered the encampment there they were, still skinning it. So I chose the dik-dik.

The dik-dik was great, real juicy and tender. Dik-dik, by the way, is a very small antelope that inhabits that particular part of the jungle.

After supper, we joined the BaMbutis around the fire. One of the men around the small bonfire slowly brought out some leaves. He placed them on a small metal disk and began to cook them over the fire. Mmn. I figured, dessert! Then he crushed the leaves up with his fingers and placed them into the bowl of a very, very long pipe. He lit the tobacco and inhaled slowly.

A familiar scent hovered above us in the dark jungle night air.

He then proceeded to pass the pipe around. I—well, once the pipe came to me, I—

She inhales the smoke and chokes.

Jesus! The Rastafarians have nothing on the pygmies.

While the pipe is doing the rounds, I notice that across the burning fire from me one of the BaMbuti men is doing something real peculiar to the two small branches he's holding. He keeps splitting the branches to a point halfway down its length, until each of the branches begins to resemble a kind of rough hand broom. Then he starts knocking one branch against the other and it makes a kind of rattling percussive sound. His rhythm is slow but precise. Then he begins to sing and in no time the rest of the clan joins him.

The BaMbuti chant is heard.

And oh, the melodies and harmonies they created were just so— I'd never heard anything like it. Underscored by the rattling percussive rhythm they were building this pyramid, in song.

Suddenly I had a brainstorm. I knew a song that came from the jungle—I had heard it so many times in the *Tarzan* movies. So, I just start singing:

Won di
Won di eh my heh oh.

Won di
Won di eh my heh oh.

Won di
Won di eh my heh oh.

Well they don't get it. So I figure, like, maybe I'm in the wrong key. In the *Tarzan* movies they always sang it really high, and I just figured that it was because they were actually southern Black Baptists in drag.

Won di
Won di eh my heh oh.

Won di
Won di eh my heh oh.

Won di...

They just didn't recognize it at all, much less like it.

Listening to BaMbuti music is like a lesson in the true forms of jazz improvisation and harmonies. Everyone has their own part and knows exactly where they fit in.

Meanwhile, recovering from my first attempt at cross-cultural communication, I remember another song, this one an actual BaMbuti chant that I learned in school. I figured they'd be really choked to hear this coming from my mouth:

Dja dja dja dja,
Mchok mdja.
Dja,
Mchok mdja

Dja dja dja dja,
Mchok mdja.
Dja,
Mchok Mdja.

Well... they didn't know this one either—but they really liked it. At first they sang the words wrong, but they soon hooked into the rhythm of the chant.

MAN ONE *and* MAN TWO *join her.*

ALL   Dja dja dja dja,
Mchok mdja.

Dja dja dja dja,
Mchok mdja.
Dja.
Mchok Mdja.

And we didn't stop singing that song for about twenty minutes.

BaMbuti music is—heavenly, yes, that's the word—just plain heavenly.

While they were singing, I began to think, that well, I should at least sing them a song from Canada, a song that rang with the true essence of Canadiana. But I couldn't think of one. It was like every Canadian song that I had ever learned leapt out of my brain and choose that particular moment to do it. A Canadian song... Canadian song... Canadian song...

Singing.

Oh Canada, our home and native land.
True patriot love, in all thy sons command.
With...

Now, I don't know whether it was a side effect of the particular brand of tobacco that we'd been smoking, but I was getting this sixth sense that they weren't really, well, liking it. So trusting my instincts and subordinating reason:

She sings the anthem like an intense soulful gospel ballad.

With glowing hearts,
We see these rise,
The true north strong and free.
From far and wide,

Oh oh oh Canadaah,
We stand on guard for thee-e-e-e.
Ohhh Canadaaaaaaaah,
Gloooorious and freeee-e-eee-e
We stand on guard, we stand on guard
For theeeeeee.
Oooohhhh Caaa-naa-daaaahhh.
We stand on Guaaaaard for-or or
Theee-ee-e-he-e-e-e-heee.

Well, they just loved it.

That night, I slept in the encampment. They offered us their huts
for the night, they are so kind. So we offered them our tents. And
as I lay in my sleeping bag on the straw mat, I began to think: here
I am in a BaMbuti hut, in the middle of the Ituri Rainforest, in
Zaire, in Africa, on the planet Earth, the third planet from the
sun in the Milky Way, situated in an unknown quadrant of the
universe—in what? What comes after universe? What's the universe in? And why was being here so special? And—I couldn't
figure it out, except that, it had something to do with—

*She sings a phrase of the anthem slowly, again in a soulful gospel
style.*

From far and wide…

That's it! See, that's me! The African heartbeat in a Canadian song.

African Canadian. Not coloured, or Negro…
Maybe not even Black. African Canadian.

And I close my eyes, and even though I had to have my legs
protruding from the doorway of the hut, because their huts are
so small, I began to feel right at home.

The airport reappears.

AIRPORT ANNOUNCER ONE

Mr. Benoit Akonde paging Miss Janet Sears. Would Miss Janet
Sears please pick up the courtesy telephone at the Air Afrique
ticket counter.

The courtesy telephone rings. DJANET *slowly moves toward it,
pauses for a moment and then picks up the receiver.*

DJANET

Hi Ben…

Mon cher, c'est n'est pas a faute de toi. C'est parce que…. Look,
I'm going to have to speak to you in English, *mon petit.…* Okay, is
this slow enough for you… but I tried to explain everything in the
letter.

Pause.

Ben, I cannot just be your wife. I must have something of my own, too. Maybe I need to tell people about what I've seen here. There are lots of people back home who need to hear about this place, who need to hear how important they are. Maybe that's it... I am an African, Ben, an African of the Americas. I belong to the African diaspora. Africa will always be here for me... I know, I know you might not be...

Pause.

Come with me, Ben. I'm serious, come with me.... Shit, we'll move to Quebec...

Pause.

Silly, of course I'll write you... I said, do not be so silly, of course I will write to you... I don't think customs allows mangoes through the post, sweetheart... I didn't forget it, I left the T-shirt there for you. And every time someone asks you what CityTV means—

AIRPORT ANNOUNCER ONE

This is a final boarding call for all passengers on Air Afrique Flight 735 en route to Paris, London, New York, and Buffalo. Would all passengers on Air Afrique Flight 735 please proceed to gate number nine.

She looks in the direction of the gate, and then back again at the telephone in her hand.

DJANET

Ben—

She hesitates.

They're calling my flight... I... okay? Yeah, you take care of yourself too. Yeah... I love you too, Benoit Viton Akonde. I love you too.

She pauses for a moment, then replaces the receiver.

I was going home—to Canada. Yeah. I had all my history on my back. The base of my whole culture would be forever with me. And funny thing is, it always had been. In my thighs, my behind, my hair, my lips.

She goes to pick up her hand luggage.

Did you know that the Sphinx's nose had originally been Negroid— No. Did you know that the Sphinx's nose had originally been African and that when the first European scientific mission found it in the nineteenth century, they chopped the Sphinx's nose off.

Michael Jackson chopped his nose off too. It's true!

Singing.

(very slow, soulful rubato) Young, gifted and Black...

(in tempo) There were times when I felt so insecure
Never sure
Where I fit in.
So I tried to be more like someone else
But it left me feeling empty inside

No matter what people say to me,
I've got to find my own way to be,
My own way to be:

Inside my African heart
Beats a special part
That gives me strength, gives *me life.*
Inside my African soul
Is where I found the light
That makes me feel right, makes me whole.

Now I know where to look to find myself.
I need someone to share their love with me
But I've got to find my own way to be,
my own way to be:

Inside my African heart
Beats a special part
That gives me strength, gives me life.
Inside my African soul
Is where I found the light
That makes me feel right, makes me whole.

Inside. Inside...

A powerful West African rhythm emerges.

In-a-side, in-a-side, in-a-side,
In-a-side in my soul.

In-a-side, in-a-side, in-a-side,
In-a-side in my soul.

Inside. Inside...

*DJANET turns in the direction of the departure gate but catches
her own reflection in an imaginary glass door in the waiting
area. She stares at herself. She adjusts her T-shirt and wrap,
then reaches into the cloth bag and pulls out a brilliantly
embroidered West African boubou. She realizes that if she*

doesn't hurry she'll miss her flight, but takes the time to make the boubou look just right.

The cloth bag is now empty. DJANET *unknots it, revealing the original length of West African fabric. She wraps the fabric around her head.*

She stares intensely at her reflection. She smiles.

You know sometimes when you look into the mirror and you sorta—catch your own I.

She sings the Carmen Jones *song in her own Canadian/ Caribbean/British style over the intense African rhythm.*

That's love
That's love
That's love
That's love

The music stops abruptly. Her metamorphosis is now complete.

Dorothy Dandridge, eat your heart out, I am beautiful.

Blackout.

In the blackout, MAN ONE *and* MAN TWO *begin a Sunnu rhythm on the cow bells, djun-djun, and djembe. As the lights come up for the curtain calls,* DJANET, MAN ONE, *and* MAN TWO *sing, releasing the incantation and ending the play.*

Ay yeh denumba,
Acoe,
Bena bee sema roe,
Dumumba.

Ay yeh denumba,
Acoe,
Bena bee sema roe,
Dumumba.

Repeat.

Curtain.

Djanet Sears is an award-winning playwright and director and has several acting award nominations to her credit for both stage and screen. She is the recipient of the Stratford Festival's 2004 Timothy Findley Award, as well as Canada's highest literary honour for dramatic writing: the 1998 Governor General's Literary Award. Other honours include the 1998 Floyd S. Chalmers Canadian Play Award, the Martin Luther King Jr. Achievement Award, the Harry Jerome Award for Excellence in the Cultural Industries, and a Phenomenal Woman of the Arts Award. Her most recent work for the stage, *The Adventures of a Black Girl in Search of God* (Playwrights Canada Press, 2003), was shortlisted for a 2004 Trillium Book Award. Her other plays include *Who Killed Katie Ross* and *Double Trouble*. Djanet is the driving force behind the AfriCanadian Playwrights' Festival, and a founding member of the Obsidian Theatre Company. She is currently an adjunct professor at University College, University of Toronto where she teaches playwriting.

Come Good Rain

To Auntie Gladys:
in loving memory
from little "Bunika, mwana wa nyoko."

Special acknowledgements go to Beth Mannion, Katrina Goldstone, Margo Nungent, Matthew Torney, and Daudi Kutta. As we say in Luganda: *Mwebale nyo*, thank you so very much.

Come Good Rain had its debut at Toronto's Factory Theatre Studio Café in February 1992, funded by the Ontario Arts Council. It was produced by Jim Millan and Crow's Theatre as part of the Flying Solo series. George Seremba played himself and all other characters.

Dramaturge/Director	Sue Miner
Musician	Emmanuel Mugerwa
Stage manager	George Athans
Lighting design	Peter Cochron
Production assistants	Kathleen Lantos
	Paula Lind

The playwright would like to gratefully acknowledge financial assistance from the Toronto Arts Council and the Canada Council for the Arts, as well as the following individuals for dramaturgical and other help: Michael Miller, Robert Rooney, Alex Mackenzie Gray, Rita Davies, Stephanie Bennett, and Christine Seremba.

— • —

Come Good Rain subsequently opened at the Samuel Beckett Theatre in Dublin on May 17, 2005. It was produced by Elizabeth Mannion and Momboze Productions. George Seremba played himself and all other characters.

Percussion	Matt Torney
Girl's voice	Nakku Makubuya
Lighting design	Michael Canney
Associate producers	Barbara Nealon
	Tara Carr

The playwright would like to thank Ben Brogan, Daudi Kutta/Diverse Eireann, and Paul Farren.

Uganda

The Republic of Uganda is situated on the equator in the east-central part of Africa. Neighbouring countries include Zaire to the west, Sudan to the north, Kenya to the east, and Tanzania and Rwanda to the south. Its capital is Kampala.

Languages: Speakers of Bantu languages account for 65% of the total population and occupy the south and west of Uganda. Speakers of Eastern Sudanic languages occupy the remainder. English is the common language of inter-ethnic communication as well as Luganda, and Swahili is also used as a *lingua franca*.

History:

1882–1962	Under British Colonial rule.
1962	The kabaka (king) of Buganda, Sir Edward Frederick Mutesa II, is elected president.
1966	Apollo Milton Obote deposes the president and establishes a one-party state.
1971	Idi Amin Dada, the commander of the armed forces, deposes Obote, is installed as president, and over the next few years begins a reign of terror that destroys the political and economic fabric of the country. The Asian population is expelled.
1978	Amin wages war on neighbouring Tanzania. The Tanzanian army and Ugandan opposition groups fight back and eventually capture Kampala and Amin flees in April 1979.
1980	Obote re-assumes the presidency after a fraudulent election. He picks up where he left off: presiding over a hegemonic and murderous regime. Obote is overthrown by his one-time cohorts including Paulo Muwanga and Bazilio Olara-Okello.
1986	Yoweri Kaguta Museveni and his National Resistance Army overthrow the cohorts, ending the terror and introducing widespread reforms. However, he inherits a devastated country—a far cry from the Uganda once described as the "pearl of Africa."
2008	President Museveni has been in power for twenty-two years. This includes the pre-new-Constitution years. So far, there is no sign he will relinquish power; Museveni appears to be in relentless pursuit of a fourth term, and what could well be a life presidency. His once heroic legacy may well have been washed away by his latter-day narrative. There is also a lot of talk about a dynastic succession(s), should he ever decide he has had enough.
2009	The September 11–13th demonstrations that engulfs Kampala and the violent response of the regime clearly demonstrates that Uganda is sadly plunged back to the future of Idi Amin and Milton Obote. A statement of this nature is now deemed to be seditious.

COME GOOD RAIN

ACT ONE

The stage is dark. A flute plays a haunting melody that will become a recurring theme throughout the play. A solitary figure makes his way through the auditorium. He's holding a candle and singing a song—or is it an incantation? Once onstage, almost ritualistically, he finds a convenient spot. He tells the story with the infectiousness of a seasoned raconteur.

GEORGE   *(singing) Abe mbuutu*
N'abe ngalabi
Banange munkubire ngenda
Mbaire yagenda nga alidda
Aligenda okudda
Nga luwedde okwaba
Mbaire yagenda nga alidda
Aligenda okudda
Nga luwedde ngenze

> "My friends play me the ceremonial drums
> Come bid me goodbye
> My father went as though he would return
> By the time he does, It will be too late
> My father went as though he would return
> By the time he does
> I will be long gone."

This is a story that old people tell. Once upon a time, a long time ago, there lived a man called Mbaire. Mbaire had a wife and two daughters. One was from an earlier marriage. Her name was Nsimb'egwire. Mbaire was also a good hunter. His expeditions sometimes took him away for many a day and many a night.

Nsimb'egwire was a humble teen. She was the talk and pride of the village, not only because of her breathtaking good looks, but also due to her remarkably good manners. This did not sit well with her stepmother. Her own daughter did not have much to cheer by way of any of these attributes.

It so happened once, that Mbaire set off for another one of his expeditions. Both girls were promptly summoned by the wife. The next day was market day. There would be a lot of people going to and from the marketplace. She shaved Nsimb'egwire's head with a vengeance, then smeared her with soot and ash and made sure her own daughter was clean and smart. That done, the girls were paraded by the roadside.

Unfortunately for the mother, even long before the sun set at the end of the day, each and every passerby she asked who of the two was more beautiful pointed at Nsimb'egwire in spite of all the soot and ash.

She couldn't take it anymore! She dragged the girl off into the wilderness. There she found a secluded spot, deep in the jungle, where even the herdsmen seldom ventured with their cattle. Behind the armour of thick foliage and branches she found a spot in the heart of an old passion tree. There she dug a shallow grave in which half the girl's body was buried under the sticky earth. Secure in the knowledge that the only likely company would be dreaded tropical snakes and animals, and that there would be no chance of human encounter, she abandoned her under the cover of darkness.

Condemned alive to solitary death, Nsimb'egwire waged a stubborn struggle to come out of her grave. For days and nights, come rain or steaming heat, she continued to struggle. But her energy was dissipating. Hunger and thirst made matters even worse. Now more than ever she wished her father would come home—death would obviously rear its ugly head. Sooner or later it would certainly knock on her door!

And yet she sang.

He sings.

Ani oyo
Ani oyo
Ani oyo ayita ku mutunda
Ku mutunda kuliko Nsimb'egwire
Nsimb'egwire muwala wa Mbaire Mbaire yagenda nga anadda
Aligenda okudda nga luwedde okwaba
Mbaire yagenda nga alidda
Aligenda okudda
Nga luwedde ngenze...

"*Who is that?*
Who is that?
You who happen to pass by the passion tree,

Let it be known that it harbours Nsimb'egwire.
Nsimb'egwire is Mbaire's daughter.
Mbaire left as though he would return,
but by the time he does, it will be too late.
By the time he returns,
I will be long gone."

> *Lights come on.* GEORGE *blows out his candle. He gets on his feet and plunges into his sea of memories with childish excitement and innocence.*

Strange how it all comes back. Yes, with Mother at the centre. My sisters and I would form a semicircle on the opposite side. We would start with a few proverbs, trade some puns and riddles.

Koyi Koyi
(in response) Lya!
Question: I have a wife whose house has no door. Who am I?
Answer: An egg.

Koyi Koyi
(in response) Lya!
Question: Gobo ne gobo?
Answer: That's what the cow's hoof says to the rock.

We would get into little ditties, tongue twisters, and song…

Question: *Kiiso kya mbuzi!*
Answer: *Kabaka*

Question: *Mbulira ensozi*
Answer: *Mengo*

At the climax of the evening, Mother would always tell a story. Soon, we too would try our luck centre stage. It was always a heady and enrapturing experience. But then, I must have been eight years or so when… it happened.

Dad had talked about a boarding school. One morning I heard him call, "*Bwanika! Bwanika!*" Not me! What have I done this time? "Rise and shine, George. Rise and shine tall, George." *(heaves a sigh of relief)* I liked that. It usually meant there was nothing to explain or atone for. Even if something was amiss and somebody swore, "George did it."

FATHER
Did you fill in the forms? What do they teach you at the local school? *(benign laughter)* The letter said in triplicate, remember. Province? Buganda. Country? Uganda. The two may sound alike but the kingdom of Buganda is only one province in the entire country! Date of birth? November 28, 1957. Sorry, son. Change that to 1956. That way you'll be able to start next year rather than

wait till January 1966. We will correct the mistake once you are admitted. You're tall enough, anyway. No one will bother cross-checking your age. The interview is next week.

A flute is heard: the haunting and solitary theme we heard at the beginning.

GEORGE   *(to audience)* After the interview, we stopped at Rubaga for a quick visit with grandmother. I couldn't wait to show her my brand new pair of "back to school with Bata shoes." I loved everything about her place. From the incense that hit your nostrils at the door to the spiced tea and the water from the ancient clay pot in the corner. The pictures, too, all over the wall: one of Auntie Gladys in her nurse's uniform at school in England. Good old Brother Stephen, with most of us when he came to visit last Christmas. One of me, a few years ago… fully dressed in my Adam's attire; and an eight-by-ten of Jesus Christ: complete with dark blue eyes and straight long blond hair.

I loved the people, too. It was always full of people, just like a school. You watched, learned, and did. "As long as the good Lord provides, there's always enough" was her motto.

We got back into the car, branched off at Nabunya, past the tiny Kabaka's Lake. To our immediate left stood the enormous red-brick wall that went all the way around the palace.

FATHER   You should ask your grandmother to take you for a visit next time she goes to the king's court. That's her lineage. Your great-grandmother's father was king of Buganda. Sekabaka Kalema, he was called. His daughter would later marry Semei Kakungulu. Your grandmother would be Kakungulu's eldest daugher, she, too would marry a famous man from across the Nile, Yekoniya Zirabamuzale. They would give birth to two beautiful daughters. Your Auntie Gladys and your mother.

GEORGE   *(to audience)* We stopped the car. I edged closer. Finally touched and stroked the ancient wall. My ancestors were no longer just names. They began to throb in my bones. I could touch and feel the country as though it had flesh and blood… unlike those lifeless maps of mountains, lakes, and rivers that hung in the back of the classrooms at the local elementary school at home.

Drums are heard.

FATHER   It's getting late, my son. Can't you hear the drums in the palace?

GEORGE   *(to audience)* At home that night on a distant hill, I could see the faint lights of Mugwanya Preparatory School. It all looked so far away. *(as a boy)* Moreover, it's still a whole year away. Assuming

I get in. Besides, there's something else on my mind. Tonight
I promised Mother I'd tell my first story… something simple like
"Nsanji and the Ogre." I'm sure nobody will laugh at me… even if
they do, it's only a beginning. Their turn will come… there is still
a whole year of practising, humiliation, making a fool of myself,
then one day, I'll stand up and recite…

Drums are heard.

Once upon a time there lived a man called Mbaire. Mbaire had
a wife and two daughters. One was from an earlier marriage. Her
name was Nsimb'egwire… it so happened once… yes. Death
would obviously rear its ugly head. Sooner or later, it would
certainly knock on her door! And yet she sang. She sang about
her beloved father, his absence, the trip, her rapidly deteriorating
condition, her plight. Her voice like a magical flute rode the back
of the wind that brushed through her confines.

*A loud and relentless bell is heard. The teacher takes a few
steps across the length and breadth of the class, like an army
instructor meeting the recruits in boot camp.*

TEACHER   My name is Pius Mulindwa. For those of you who do not know
me, I'll be in charge of English language and mathematics.
Welcome to Mugwanya Preparatory School, Kabojja. Many
are called but few are chosen, so you should all feel proud of
yourselves and once again… welcome. Please be seated.

He turns to the register and starts the roll call.

John Bosco Baguma, George Bwanika—please don't stand, just
say, "present, sir"—Peter Luzige… good. Joseph Mary Odongo,
Stephen Ruhinda… Paul Semazzi, David Tamale. Is there anyone
whose name is missing?

Being the class master of Primary 3B, it's my responsibility to
supervise the elections for the class monitor and one junior
prefect. *(beat)* Silence. As tomorrow's leaders and responsible
citizens, remember it's your birthright to exercise your vote.
Feel free to nominate anyone. Once they are seconded, we shall
proceed with a show of hands.

Before we do that, each of the candidates will have to come
forward and address the class. No big promises… you just tell the
class, in a minute or two, why they should vote for you.

Very well then. *(walks to the blackboard)* Fred Ma-Ku-Mbi,
seconded? Amoti Ruhun… wait a minute, what happened to your
Christian name, my boy? Good, very good, John A. Ruhundwa. No
more nominations, volunteers?

Hmm! *(aside)* I hate to see any youngsters toy with popular consensus. That is for socialists and the birds. I shouldn't worry though. They are all under thirteen. All ours, to shape and mould.

(back to the class) John and Fred, please come forward. I'm pleased to announce that the pupils of standard 3B now have a school prefect and class monitor. A round of applause for your new leaders. Very well then. Please be seated.

You have now become the eyes and ears of the school. Remember to always serve by setting a good example. Only then can you make sure the rule of law is maintained. No one is above the law, not even the prefects. Repeat after me, not even the... yes, we don't care whether you are the son of the president of the United States or even the queen of England.

Gleefully, he parades his stick.

Just don't put us to the test. Believe me, we shall pass it with flying colours. At Mugwanya Preparatory School, we have more punishments than all the rules put together.

There are a lot of people who put money in this school. Some from as far away as Canada and even the United States of America. However bright you are, if you prove too unruly, we'll ask you to put on your Sunday uniform and tell your parents that we'd be more than happy to recommend you to the reformatory school at Kampiringisa.

I have seen mothers drop on their knees and threaten to shed tears of blood.

He brandishes and strokes his cane.

Now. Lateness. Some of you actually sauntered into class like... little gazelles! From now on... latecomers eat bones. No more African time! Punctuality is a must. Punctuality is a what?

Beat. The class responds.

I notice some of you are still speaking "vernacular"! Save that for your grandmothers during the holidays. From now on you must speak English, eat English, sleep English, and dream English. You must speak...?

To audience, waits for response.

Good. Any questions? Wait a minute, George Bwanika...

He gestures for GEORGE to come forward.

Your father tells me you might need some extra help in mathematics. Make sure you report to the staff room after lunch. Are you related to Brother Stefano Bwanika? Ooh, then I must watch you with extra care. The children of the religious are the worst behaved.

He turns to the class.

Very well then. Do you all remember the song we learned this morning? Look at it and take your friends through. Are we all ready? No sissies this time. One, two, three…

He sings.

Hey diddle diddle,
The cat and the fiddle
The cow jumped over the moon.
The little dog laughed to see such fun,
The dish ran away with the spoon.

A school bell rings.

GEORGE   *(to audience)* Having gone through an entire year, I felt immensely glad that at least I was no longer a newcomer.

One Saturday afternoon I stood outside the classroom. I did not feel like playing Batman and Robin or taking a "French leave" to buy Coca-Cola or Pepsi. What should I do, I said to myself?

Mr. Mulindwa always told us that "an idle mind is a devil's workshop." I had to keep myself busy. So I sat down and looked at the sky. All of a sudden I saw a rainbow, its trunk huge and long: full of colour. I instantly found myself on my feet, as if in conspiracy with the gentle creature beyond the horizon.

He sings.

Enkuba etonya
Omusana gwaka
Engo ezala
Ezalira ku lwazi

"*The rain is falling.*
The sun is shining.
The leopard is giving birth.
It's giving birth down on a rock."

A school bell rings. GEORGE *is oblivious to it.*

Ka nemu kanabiri
Kafumba mwanyi
Kata konkome
Kalangaja ka nakwale
Ofumba otya ku lugyo

The school bell rings again. The TEACHER *arrives; he strikes one of his favourite poses.*

TEACHER	Five of the best, my boy. Thou shalt neither speak nor sing in vernacular.
GEORGE	But sir, there is no translation for that song.
TEACHER	One more stroke for every excuse you make. What's that word you used? Translation... *(fully exasperated)* Stubborn boy. If you make any more excuses, I'll multiply the strokes and put your name in the black book. Unless... when you go back to the dormitory tonight, you make me a list of all the vernacular speakers. Even the walls have ears, remember.

You have two full days for the list.

Organ music.

GEORGE	*(on his knees)* Our Father who art in Heaven. Please let me not betray anyone.

The school bell rings.

For the Kingdom the Power and the Glory is yours, forever and ever. Amen.

(to audience) Nothing short of a miracle would alter my fate. Those strokes and the big horrendous black book kept my eyes open all through the night. Suddenly, I heard bursts of gunfire in the distance. Could this be a dream?

Rapid gunfire is heard.

The whole school saw it the next morning. A cloud of thick, black smoke billowing out of the kabaka's palace at Mengo. The palace! More guns and mortars. A bit of a lull. Then it resumed until the rain fell that afternoon.

In the staff room the teachers were huddled together around the radio.

Martial music is heard.

ANNOUNCER	This is a special announcement. The recent "conflict" between the government of Buganda and the federal government has finally been resolved. His Excellency, Milton Obote, has now become the president of Uganda. None of the changes he has made can be questioned in a court of law. The old federal constitution as well as the monarchy is now null and void. Soon a new republican constitution will be in place. There will be a curfew as well as a state of emergency all over Buganda until further notice. This is not a military coup.

Martial music is heard again.

TEACHER	*(addressing* GEORGE*)* Have you got the list of vernacular speakers? No? You are forgiven. Go.

Wait. There is something to be said for your loyalty to your friends. Courage for a good cause is a good thing. Even when one has to be punished for it. Which brings me to the heart of the matter.

Just like the brothers, all of you are my children. Even if one sheep strays from the herd, why, I pick up the cane and abandon the ninety-nine.

He looks around, takes a deep breath.

I'm telling you this because listening to the radio this afternoon, I found myself asking deep and painful questions.

(pause) Why should I flog you for speaking your mother tongue, which I have the audacity to call "vernacular," when the same language or your name alone is enough to ruffle the soldiers' feathers at a roadblock? They are all over the province. Just like locusts, even in the villages from Luwero to Lwabenge, Kalisizo and beyond. See the one at the junction? Some of our own staff have already been victimized at it.

All I see is a long monstrous tunnel. At the end of it, strange and merciless beings that would have made Julius Caesar wail like a child. At their head, the new headmaster—Milton Obote—wielding a large whip.

At least my days of flogging are over. The rest is up to you. *(barely audible)* When you grow up, remember… you have a right to disagree, and maybe even make mistakes. *(shakes his head)* You are a free man, my boy.

A few shots are fired in the vicinity. He goes down on his knees.

(pause) It's far from over. The real tragedy is that we are all Africans. All Ugandans, and all just as human as those men in uniform! The landscape has changed.

GEORGE	*(to audience)* This was all too much for my little head. I looked at the teacher walking away as the rain began to fall… and I thought about Nsimb'egwire, the little girl in the proverb, all by her lonely self in the wilderness, one-eyed death staring her in the eye. And yet she sang with the hope that, by chance, a well-meaning human soul would come to her rescue. If the worst came to the worst, at least they would know who she was. Then the mbuutu and ngalabi drums would be played, the way they always do, during the last funeral rites. Unwilling to quit, she almost stubbornly continued to reach out beyond the periphery of the branches…

He sings.

Ani oyo
Ani oyo
Ani oyo ayita ku mutunda
Ku mutunda kuliko Nsimb'egwire

> *Addressing the audience, slowly, he ticks off the years on his fingers.*

One, two, three! Yet another year went. Another year came and went.

> *Drums.*

As for Obote and his UPC party loyalists, they now spoke about being in power for the next ninety-nine years. *(Drum roll. He mounts the rostrum.)* "I am the only African leader who is not scared of a military coup." *(more drums)* Outside the country, Obote had become a big hero for "poetizing" the masses, whatever that means. In January 1971, another opportunity availed itself for the dynamic "Prince of Progressive Africa" to roast the British at a Commonwealth conference in Singapore.

> *Martial music is heard. A voice comes on the radio.*

VOICE This is a special announcement. My name is Captain Aswa. We, the officers and men of the Uganda Armed Forces…

GEORGE We couldn't wait. We all struggled for a place around the current affairs notice board. Both the BBC and Voice of America confirmed it: a bloodless coup.

> *More martial music.*

VOICE And there will be a curfew in the Akokoro District. From dawn to dusk.

GEORGE *(to audience)* Dawn to dusk! Could have been a slip of the tongue. After all, the man himself was choking with emotion. So were we. Down at the Kampala-Masaka Highway, people gathered, singing, dancing, and drinking. The motorists moved at a snail's pace, some dragging and flogging Obote's effigy. Someone pulled me aside. A fellow student from 2C.

STUDENT It could be a hoax, you know.

GEORGE What?

STUDENT African presidents do it sometimes. Then arrest everyone that comes out to celebrate the fake coup.

GEORGE So why are you here? I couldn't tell where he stood on this. But it was clear he hated military coups. At least for now, I remembered

1966—Obote's pillages, rapes, murders—and could not help but join the celebration.

Ululation, as GEORGE *dances to a traditional drumbeat.*

Back at St. Henry's College, it was standing-room only, in the tiny old hall where we usually gathered for bull dances on Sunday afternoons. The television was on. The gates of the Luzira Maximum Security Prison were open. The five MPs, dubbed the Bantu Five, were free at last. Rumour had it some of them would become cabinet ministers in a matter of hours. Hundreds of other detainees were out too. The cameras were now focused on one man.

More martial music.

IDI AMIN   I, Idi Amin Dada, do solemnly swear…

GEORGE   *(to audience)* For some reason, he spoke next to no English, but we were ready to accept this gentle giant.

IDI AMIN   I am… not… a politician, but… a… professional… sodya.

GEORGE   *(to audience)* We loved this noble savage. He played the accordion and the bagpipes. They said he was a smash hit in England itself. After a sumptuous dinner, by no less a person than his ex-commander-in-chief, Africa's Big Daddy articulately stood up to express his gratitude: "I would like to completely… and… also, undress the Queen…. When you come to Uganda we shall… do it again…. Thank you."

We applauded his sincerity in those early days, and laughed—not at him—but with him. As a gesture of his magnanimity, the remains of Sir Edward Mutesa, King Freddie, would be returned from exile for the kind of funeral he deserved.

Drumbeat. GEORGE *sings the first stanza of the Ugandan national anthem.*

Oh Uganda, may God uphold thee,
We lay our future in thy hands.
United, free, for liberty,
Together we'll always stand.

Amin had another appointment with magnanimity. This one came in the form of a decree that God *(very slight pause)* air-mailed to him; by way of a dream. Accused of milking the economic cow of the country "without feeding it," the Asian community was given ninety days to leave the country. Their pockets empty, as their ancestors' had been when they built the railway.

Drum roll.

Now, to the next phase. Operation Mafuta Mingi. *(another drum roll)* In droves, people came, queued up; their ethnic and religious stripes clearly displayed. It all happened too quickly. Some people found themselves propelled from houseboys to pharmaceutical tycoons.

Then the shortages set in, and the prices quadrupled. Amin said: "Where is the governor of the national bank? Print more money or you're dead!" *(beat)* And he died.

The good old watering holes for the illicit enguli or Nubian gin really began to flourish. Every once in a while, I too would walk in and take my place among the customers for the cheap and lethal drink.

SOMEONE   Did you hear about so-and-so?

GEORGE   Yes. How sad.

(whispers to the audience) Byron Kawada was his name, playwright. Only recently he'd returned from a festival in Nigeria. Members of the State Research Bureau arrived at the National Theatre in broad daylight. For every scene he wrote, another tooth was knocked out of his gums. At the end of the exercise, his body was soaked in acid.

He points to NALONGO, *the proprietor.*

Nalongo, give us another drink. Life is too short.

(to audience) News of the latest victims would be exchanged on Radio Katwe—the grapevine telegraph through which people got the news behind the news.

SOMEONE   *(repeating the refrain)* Did you hear about so-and-so?

GEORGE surveys the place.

GEORGE   *(to audience)* Yes. How sad. It had become the refrain, this new riddle: did you hear about so-and-so?

(to NALONGO*)* Nalongo, one more please—for the road… the road of life. We might as well celebrate. Otherwise we'll die long before the trigger is pulled.

(to audience, exceptionally candid) Think about it, friends. Especially those of you who *(ironic)* may be lucky enough to have been spared the luxury of growing up in countries where no one should!

In the early days, the sight of a dead body on your way to school was something you talked about for a long time to come. Time passed. Things changed. We found ourselves haunted by images of people shot and abandoned for the vultures. Men with their genitals stuffed into their mouths like Cuban cigars. Others burnt with acid. Pregnant women; bellies ripped apart by bayonets. Alleged foes, naked and chained, paraded on national television before facing a firing squad. *(turns back to audience)* Eh... did you hear about so-and-so?

Pause. He stands and walks away.

Yes? How sad indeed.

My watering hole visits were reduced now because of my obligations—studies at the university and rehearsals for a play. But the last time I had been, Nalongo, the bartender, had told me about her daughter. The daughter was dating a soldier. The soldier had money and she wanted him to take her shopping. One day, the daughter got her wish.

NALONGO   The soldier said she'd bugged him too much so he drove her to Namanve Forest.

SOLDIER   You said you wanted to shop. Let's go.

NALONGO   It was already dark so he flashed a torch and led her deeper into the forest. They arrived, and there they were: piles of dead bodies all over, some only newly unloaded, some only dead for a matter of hours. He ordered her to have her pick from shoes to handbags, watches and necklaces. He forced her to load the trunk with valuables, and dropped her home.

GEORGE   At least she's alive.

NALONGO   But she's joined the living dead!

GEORGE   *(to audience)* We all kept quiet except for one gentleman who stood up and said:

CUSTOMER   Today it's me, tomorrow it's you! They can't go on killing us yesterday and mounting our daughters tomorrow. When my turn comes, I'll tell them you can take my body but not my spirit.

GEORGE   *(to audience)* A few months later our play, *The Fire Spreads*, opened at the National Theatre. A different kind of fire was spreading. During the second act, I was backstage putting my costume on when all of a sudden, we heard a thunder-like sound. The theatre was instantly half empty. More deafening sounds. *(makes the sound of mortar shells exploding)* The Tanzanian army and the Ugandan exiles were closing in on both Kampala and Entebbe.

Eight years and five hundred thousand deaths later, Idi Amin had finally fallen. A new provisional government was in power. The nightmare was over.

He sings.

Bewayo abaana bebazibwa
Ku lwaffe bawayo obulamu
N'ebyona

Babasulaamu amabomu
Babakuba na amasasi
Babatemamu
Obufififi bona…

> "*Our selfless children who sacrificed themselves are hereby applauded.*
> *For us they gave their lives.*
> *And all.*
> *They were showered with bombs,*
> *Drilled with bullets.*
> *Hacked into pieces…*"

Sixty-eight days later, Professor Lule, the first provisional president, was put under house arrest and sent into exile. Milton Obote's stalwarts now appeared in prominent government posts. The honeymoon was over.

For us, it was a time to scream if that's the only way we could be heard. Men, women, and children—with the women at the forefront, some with their babies strapped to their backs—all took to the streets singing:

Fe twagala Lule
Oba tuffa tuffe
Atamwagala agende

> "*We love Lule,*
> *We love him to death.*
> *Those that hate him should leave the country.*"

The soldiers gathered around them all over the city, from Nile Mansions to City Square and Entebbe Road. Their guns did the talking.

The sound of gunfire.

But the massacres did not stop us. All around the city, barricades were mounted and fires lit. My friend Richard and I were at the forefront of the demonstrations and against the return of Obote. There was no turning back. We both knew it. We gathered a few friends and at night littered the city with pamphlets to keep the voice of protest alive.

Campus politics, too, were now fully revived. Lumumba Hall was our first experiment. Through some kind of alliance, all of our candidates came to power in a resounding victory. The University Guild presidency was next. Me, who had never held a single office in my school years, had all of a sudden been propelled into a spokesperson for the voices of dissent.

If Obote ever returns to power, that will be the time for me to become a Sandinista.

In the afternoon, I get into Lumumba Hall, and a custodian friend hastily beckons me to the desk.

CUSTODIAN   *(whispers)* The bad boys were here. Intelligence officers, probably from Impala House. Asked for your name and room number. Actually went up and waited for a long while.

GEORGE   Hmm. *(beat)* Didn't know I was that important to them. Keep it to yourself. I'll lie low for a while… make myself more scarce.

(to audience) Then came news that Gasta Nsubuga, a prominent businessman, who had funded a great deal of our Guild presidency campaign, was shot. Rushed to hospital by his family, they shot him again—in his hospital bed! But he still defied death. His family finally smuggled him across the border to a Kenyan hospital. Obote's well-oiled machine was getting stronger and more vicious by the day. Lameck Ntambi, another popular politician, was the next target. I helped him escape. *(pause)* Who will the next target be?

Obote himself has finally landed on Ugandan soil. It is time for me to go and lie low, in some kind of self-imposed exile, across the border in Nairobi.

In Nairobi, I saw Robert Serumaga. The Ugandan playwright-, actor-, and director-turned-freedom-fighter was one of those that were sent back into exile only sixty-eight days after they helped overthrow Idi Amin. Noble, humorous, generous, almost to a fault. I remember asking him once: "How about another play?" He replied, "I'm in a play right now, except, in this one, the main characters must die."

And he died. A brutal and tragic death that raised questions about foul play and betrayal. I turned to his friend, David Rubadiri, and through him, I started teaching school in Kilungu.

School bell rings.

My name is George Bwanika. I'll be in charge of English language as well as literature and drama.

Bell rings again.

(to audience) Although I did take to Kilungu like a fish to water, I found myself homesick within no time. On November twenty-eighth, I would be twenty-two. The prospect of having my first Christmas away from my family was far from endearing.

The elections in Uganda were hardly a fortnight away. "Take advantage of the confusion," I said to myself. "Soon the elections will be over, and should Obote be firmly entrenched, it's going to be far more difficult to enter—let alone leave—the country!" I decided to go home for Christmas.

As the bus approached the border before the crack of dawn on the fifth of December, I began to have serious doubts about my decision.

There were rumours of lists and pictures on the Ugandan end. My heart was throbbing like a drum as I whispered my last prayer before going through Ugandan customs and immigration... and... bingo! I had gone through both in record time. I was standing firmly on Ugandan soil.

> *A haunting flute theme is heard. It is the same tune as the Nsimb'egwire song.*

A few days later we drove towards Kampala. The closer we got to Kampala, the more tense I felt. This was election day. Minutes after my arrival at the campus, Paulo Muwanga, one of Obote's stalwarts, issued a disturbing proclamation.

MUWANGA   *(as if in a studio, savouring his power and arrogance)* Nobody is allowed to release the election results except *(slight pause, but the comedy does not obscure the eeriness)* me. If you are caught doing so, you will either pay a fine of half-a-million shillings or go to prison for five years, or both.

GEORGE   That evening as I walked towards Lumumba Hall, a student I once considered a friend confronted me with great hostility.

STUDENT   Why didn't you stay and vote back in Moi's Kenya?

GEORGE   *(to audience)* I was with two undergraduate friends of mine who remained quiet. Their party, the DP, had already won seventy percent of the seats, unofficially.

STUDENT   Why didn't you stay and vote in Moi's Kenya?

GEORGE   *(annoyed)* I do not bandy words with fools. I don't even have the time to waste. *(to audience)* There was a ferociousness in his tone and eyes. He walked away, accompanied by a chorus of derisive laughter. *(slight pause)* As we approached Lumumba Hall...

> *He starts to walk, stops, and addresses the two friends.*

Do you see what I see? Two military Jeeps! Hmm. Under cover of darkness they won't know who we are. Okay, wait here.

He walks ahead.

(to himself) They are empty. But there are a lot of soldiers right at the main gate to the hall.

He looks through a window.

They seem to be splitting into little groups, traversing the corridors, and knocking on doors! Who are they looking for? I'll make just one more stop to see John and his wife and then out of the campus. *(to his friends)* Bye. I'll see you tomorrow.

(to audience) I turned right... before I got to the mango tree in John's courtyard I could hear voices of celebration. Pronouncement or no pronouncement, nobody would rob them of their victory.

In the distance drums, victorious chanting, clinking glasses, ululation, etc., are heard; the volume rises as GEORGE *approaches.*

John worked on the switchboard in the main hall, and ran a little shebeen on the side. He and his wife were friends to a great many of us. Despite his blindness, he knew most of us almost by sight.

GEORGE   *(At the door. Knocks.)* John, it's...

JOHN   Don't tell me it's you, George. Come in... come in. We are so glad to see you.

GEORGE   *(to audience)* I had never seen John that happy. Except for a head-bowed medical student in a corner, it was so wild and euphoric you would think Idi Amin had just fallen.

The crowd swells even more.

CROWD   Welcome back. *(He ululates.)* Welcome back from exile.

GEORGE   *(to audience)* Some of them had always been intimate friends. Some had actually nicknamed me "Okigbo"—after the Nigerian poet, a name I would never have escaped if my fellow "penguins," as the literature students were called, got wind of it.

CROWD   *(chanting) Umuofia Kwenu... Uganda Kwenu...* DP, *hoye... hoye,* UPM, *hoye hoye.* CP, *hoye...* UPC... *chini... chini, Obote zii... zi zaidi.*

GEORGE   *(to audience)* Not a glass or a single bottle was idle. They were also rubbing it in, but as if on a mission, the man in the corner appeared unruffled and determined to stay. I also had my say, appropriately quoting from Achebe's *Things Fall Apart:* "We do

not wish to hurt anybody, but if anybody wishes to hurt us, may
he break his neck."

(Sits. Looks at his watch.) I have to leave for Kasubi in the next five
minutes.

(to audience) I reluctantly accept John's drink. For some reason
I just haven't felt like drinking at all. Nine o'clock. It's time to say
goodbye.

 Looks at his watch again. A menacingly loud knock on the door.

(to audience) Before John opens the door, two people walk in; one
is an armed soldier, the other a student in Obote's UPC party
colours.

FIRST SOLDIER Who here is George Bwanika?

GEORGE *(to audience)* Everybody has instantly sobered up. You can almost
hear the silence. A round of silence.

 His inner voice takes over.

How long do you think they will manage without revealing your
identity? Look as normal as they are George… whatever that
means. *(to audience)* The man in the corner no longer has his
head bowed. He looks very calm and unthreatened. *(inner voice;
cold and calculated instinct)* Grab him, he is within easy reach.
You have the speed and power to hurl him in front of the soldier.
Remember there is a seldom-used door to your immediate left.
Don't be afraid. Grab him by surprise, he will give you cover, then
jump as soon as you open the door. What if it's locked, though?!

(to audience; still glued to his seat) A second soldier walks in, and
I abandon the option.

(reverts to his thoughts) Sooner than later someone is going to
point me out. True, they did welcome me back from exile, but
there is a limit to a lot of things. Then there is this pretentiously
quiet man in the corner. If nobody points me out, he will.

SECOND SOLDIER All of you produce your identity cards.

 *Pregnant pause. Through a quick lighting change there is a
spotlight on GEORGE as he pulls his card from his pocket. He
drops it on the floor, steps on it, and then slides it downstage
as if underneath a bench. He pulls out his diary, flips through it.
Satisfied, he slides it under the bench with his left leg. It's now
his turn.*

GEORGE Sorry. I inadvertently forgot to carry mine. Didn't know it was
a necessary prerequisite within the confines of the campus.

	(to audience) This was a bit of a loop. None of them could identify George Bwanika. To make matters worse, they expected him to simply stand up and say "present, sir"—just like we used to do at school. They turned to John and his wife.
SECOND SOLDIER	*Ako wapi?* Where is he?
JOHN	I'm afraid it would be very hard for me to…
GEORGE	*(to audience)* He's slapped across the face.
SECOND SOLDIER	Who here is George Bwanika?
JOHN	*(angry and courageous)* I'm not expected to know every student who passes through here. Listen, I just run a business. Besides, I'm totally blind. I can't see. I strictly rely on voices which I sometimes confuse.
SECOND SOLDIER	What about you? You are this man's wife. Where is he?
WIFE	I stand by my husband's words.
	The SOLDIER *slaps her.*
GEORGE	*(to* SOLDIER, *quickly retrieving his card)* I quickly retrieved my card. Here. It's me.
FIRST SOLDIER	What have you come back to do here?
GEORGE	*(aside, to audience)* This is ridiculous. Isn't Uganda my country too?! *(to* SOLDIER*)* I came back just like any other Ugandan would… especially so because of the elections. I thought it was time for me, too, to chip in and do my part in the enormous task of rehabilitation. Regardless of whoever came to power after the free and fair elections, of course. If you have any doubts about what I say, ask the Department of Literature or Music, Dance, and Drama, they will fill you in.
SECOND SOLDIER	*Sumama!*
	GEORGE *flings himself to his feet.*
FIRST SOLDIER	Face the wall.
SECOND SOLDIER	He wants to somersault!
FIRST SOLDIER	Walk to the corner.
	GEORGE *does so.*
	There. Sit down! *(slight pause before the* SOLDIER *starts hitting* GEORGE*)* Do you deny that we have seen you in Nairobi? Do you deny that we have seen you in Nairobi with certain exiles?
GEORGE	I have lots of friends and relatives in Nairobi… but if you… expect more answers take me to whoever your boss is… so at least I know that…

FIRST SOLDIER   You really want to meet the boss?

GEORGE   *(to audience)* What else could I say? With my blood slowly trickling down to the floor, the best I could do was buy a little more time. Better going to prison anyway. Word gets around. My friends will try getting me out even before my family gets the news. I turned to the rest for one last look. Outside, another medical student was standing guard. He nodded to confirm that they had the right man, then raised his left hand and six more soldiers emerged. They had made an extended line outside the house. My hands were up. All around me a spectacular ring of gun muzzles. As we turned towards Lumumba Hall…

STUDENT   Who is that?

GEORGE   I knew the voice. It was Mr. "Why-didn't-you-vote-in-Moi's-Kenya?" himself.

STUDENT   Agh. That one. You just kill.

       End of Act One.

ACT TWO

A few minutes later.

FIRST SOLDIER *(thick north Ugandan accent)* Sasa we lia kama mbugi.

    GEORGE bleats like a goat.

Stop. Now you laugh.

    GEORGE laughs wildly.

Stop. Now you cry like a cow.

    GEORGE ends up bellowing like a bull.

Stop. Now you bark like a dog.

    GEORGE barks.

Now you cry… stop.

    GEORGE continues moaning.

Stop!!

GEORGE *(to audience)* I stopped. So too did my hopes of striking a human chord.

With me spread-eagled on the floor of one of the military vehicles, we made our way through the speed bumps and potholes that filled the streets. I was a doormat to their thick boots.

    He tries to absorb the hits in a spread-eagled stance. He takes and discards his position as occasion demands it.

Sometimes the butts of their guns would have a little dialogue with my ribs. The first soldier, who was the leader, issued orders quietly, his pistol keeping my wrists busy.

A blinding flood of lights hit my face. This was Nile Mansions, the five-star hotel where the top brass lived and worked, indulged themselves and felt more secure than living among the real people.

FIRST SOLDIER *Toa viatu. ("Take off your shoes.")*

GEORGE *(takes off his shoes)* The walk into the building was an interesting display—you should have seen it, a soldier at the back, one at the front as well, all around us imaginary foes that kept them busy.

FIRST & SECOND SOLDIERS

He wants to somersault. He wants to somersault. He wants…

GEORGE Me in the middle, encaged in this now-familiar and spectacular island of steel and human hands. Definitely more protected than any "President for Life."

SECOND SOLDIER Have you been to Israel?

GEORGE	The voice sounded almost friendly.
SECOND SOLDIER	Have you been to Israel?
GEORGE	*(not answering the SOLDIER)* I couldn't help but smile looking at him… were they more afraid than I? Did they think they were that important? One doesn't have to go to Tel Aviv to fight this ragtag bunch. Still, I would neither confirm nor deny.
	We finish the final flight of stairs, pass through a door into what looks like the outer chamber of a bigger office. Less than a year ago someone was killed in this building, I recall. A teenage girl. Her father—a cabinet minister—was at work down the street. They said it was a stray bullet that did it. There tend to be a lot of those when certain governments are changing in Africa. The office is full of gadgets. A uniformed figure sits behind a huge desk.
FIRST SOLDIER	*(Clicks his heels. Executes a quick salute.)* We have brought him. The man who had come to cause chaos at Makerere.
GEORGE	*(to audience)* I had finally met the boss. No less a man than Brigadier David Oyite-Ojok. His name alone made the blood of many a Ugandan freeze.
	"Sir…" I struggled through bleeding lips. His eyes were so small they looked like little slits… so red, more red than they used to look on television. He looks tired. Ruthlessly cold. Insensitive. *(to Brigadier Oyite-Ojok)* Sir… some of my friends and relatives fought alongside you during the struggle against Amin.
	No response.
FIRST SOLDIER	Do you deny that you escaped from prison?
GEORGE	Sir, I have never been to prison. Which prison?
FIRST SOLDIER	You were supposed to be in prison, anyway. We have it in your file.
GEORGE	*(to audience)* The boss gestured for him to take this "walking blasphemy" out of his office. I was shoved onto a small balcony.
FIRST SOLDIER	Talk! Talk! Talk! Talk, you bloody bandit! Do you deny that we have seen you in Nairobi? Do you deny that we have seen you in Nairobi with certain exiles? Talk. Talk. Name them.
GEORGE	I knew which name they wanted most: Robert Serumaga, the playwright, buried in a foreign land. Cause of death: dubious. Even in his death I couldn't betray him. All I could say was *(mutters)* "Let his soul rest in peace."
	I could have dropped a few names of prominent exiles who were still alive. Every silent response earned me another blow, but the pain was more and more distant. I had reduced my body to an

empty husk. Now I was a little bird perched on a little branch witnessing perhaps what mankind enjoys most.

After a few more blows, he resolves to say something.

(facing the SOLDIERS*)* Thank you…. Thank you…. Thank you.

FIRST SOLDIER   *(disturbed)* Why are you thanking us? Why are you…?

GEORGE   Because you know what you are doing.

There is a beat. SOLDIER *laughs menacingly.*

(to audience) His friend returned with an ashtray full of burning cigarette butts.

FIRST SOLDIER   Bend forward. Put your chin on your knees.

GEORGE   They were stuffed into my shirt. All over my back. I remembered a story about a Greek Cypriot mercenary on the eve of his execution somewhere in Africa. His sister, who'd visited him in prison, couldn't bear to say goodbye. She broke down and wept. All he would say was "Never let them see you cry, remember you are a Greek." A youthful officer approached the scene.

OFFICER   What has he done?

Silence.

GEORGE   *(turns to him)* Sir, among other things, they are accusing me of having escaped from lawful custody. But I have never been to jail.

OFFICER   *(cautious reprimand)* You should not take such drastic steps if you don't have enough evidence.

FIRST SOLDIER   *Chacha hi mkubwa nasema nini? ("What the hell is this boss saying?")*

GEORGE   *(to audience)* It was as though this was the stupidest statement they'd ever heard. They were enraged. They dragged me back into the inner chamber. Promptly explained everything in their mother tongue. The "almighty" Ojok issued some rapid orders and took a good long look at me.

Back at the waiting vehicle the soldier with the friendly tone leaned over to brief the one in the driver's seat.

SECOND SOLDIER   He says kill!

GEORGE   Lord, now lettest thou thy servant depart in peace.

GEORGE *assumes the spread-eagled position once again.*

(to SOLDIERS*)* Gentlemen, since I do not have that much time left, can you please allow me a final look at the moon and the stars? *(Sits. Begs for a little more.)* And please don't hit me as hard. All

you'll do is deprive me of the pain in the end. If you don't mind, I'll say my last prayers.

> *He tilts his head skyward, arms together, and begins his secret prayers.*

Two things, good Lord…. One, these men have humiliated me a great deal; when the moment comes let me not go like a coward. If nobody else sees my body, at least let my mother see it so she does not spend the rest of her life thinking I'll one day show up. Do shorten the family's grief, Lord, and give them as long and as safe a life as possible.

FIRST SOLDIER	Lie down.
GEORGE	I could tell we had reached the major roadblock at Ntinda.
SECOND SOLDIER	*(at the checkpoint)* We are members of the G branch. We are on a mission and we shall be back soon. Thank you.
GEORGE	*(to audience)* And so we went, through Banda, Kireka, Bweyogerere, and finally stopped in the middle of the road. This was the famous Namanve Forest, the place where many Ugandans met their deaths. The place where Nalongo's daughter went shopping.

The soldier with the friendly tone pulled me aside. He was a bit of a giant and reminded me of the noble savage in Swift's voyage to Brobdingnag.

SECOND SOLDIER	You refused to talk, so now… you will talk when it is too…
GEORGE	When the bullets begin to flower.
SECOND SOLDIER	Take off your watch. What about the money… is this all you have?
GEORGE	I wish you'd told me before… I would have given you more but I left it at John's place, tucked in my little diary.
SECOND SOLDIER	Where?
GEORGE	In a corner below the bench I was on.
SECOND SOLDIER	You have a diary…? Anyway, we have to go back and pick up two students who were seen in your company.
GEORGE	*(to himself)* Thank God they weren't with me at John's. Thank God the soldiers are going back there, though; now at least people will know and spread news of my tragedy.
	(to audience) For a moment I thought about Dora Bloch, the elderly Israeli woman who was dragged from Mulago Hospital when the Israelis rescued their hostages at Entebbe. What were her last thoughts? Her remains were finally discovered not too far

from here. "Do not let them see your tears… remember you are a Greek."

The front door opened for the mean little boss who'd called the shots all the way from Makerere. He stuck his pistol in my lower ribs.

FIRST SOLDIER   Escort me.

GEORGE   Excuse me, could you please not shoot me through the back? I would prefer to look at you while you shoot. Thank you. *(takes a few short steps)*

(internal) Goodbye, Mum, I owe you an apology for overstaying this night on the campus. Goodbye, Dad. Goodbye, my lovely sisters, Abby, little Tony, every single one of you. Remember he loved you all and loved his country.

(Stops. To SOLDIERS.) Is this okay? Could you please give me a minute or two to say my last words? Now that you have come to power through the ballot box and not the barrel of a gun, even if I had committed a treasonable offence, you should at least have taken me to prison or a court of law. I know it's too late for me to live, but whoever continues to live in your country will find it hard to forgive, let alone forget. I am ready.

(to audience) So were they, except for the "noble savage."

SECOND SOLDIER   No, I am not shooting, but you can use my gun.

GEORGE   *(internal)* Oh, Robert Serumaga, what would you have done? Give me strength to go through this.

A gun goes off.

(to audience) The first bullet had hit the right leg. I was down on my knees… actually squatted. Before I knew it, the left arm was grazed.

Another shot is heard.

The body was now contorted as another got a bit of skin just above the forehead. But this time the body moved back and forth, never still and unwilling to give them a clean shot at the chest or the stomach.

Yet another shot is let go.

The next one found my right hand at an angle just over my heart.

Bang.

It felt big compared to the tiny needle-like sensations, as though it entered with a vengeance. Then another through the right thigh.

A fifth shot is fired.

There was a brief lull. Someone picked up my "friend's" gun. It was a rocket-propelled grenade. There was a grin on his face as he put the gun over his shoulder. I stared at him in disbelief. Oh, God there goes the rest of the body.

The deafening sound of a small rocket-propelled grenade is heard.

A big bolt-like cluster of sharp little machetes had drilled through my thigh… I was on my back, the feet were burning, there were a few flames and a pungent smell. I rolled backwards. I could see a little thicket and some undergrowth to my immediate left, a bit of a ditch as well.

The familiar, and by now comparatively tame, sound of another bullet is heard.

A solid bullet went through my left ankle as I rolled over.

An instantaneous barrage of bullets.

The AK-47s were now on rapid-fire. There was lead all around me… sort of like popcorn. The AK-47s were quite clearly on rapid-fire.

Another stomach-churning barrage.

I had landed in a shallow stream or marsh. I could smell the clay. Except for the head, I had practically sunk. There was still one crucial bullet. The one I wouldn't see. The one that would end it all. The one that would enter through the back of my head.

Shooting ends as suddenly as it had begun.

It is quiet. Frighteningly quiet.

(Very quietly. Internal.) Be still, George, still as a stone. What are they up to? God, let it not be that they are planning to cut the head off the corpse to show their boss! Or simply dump my body in the lake or the Nile: the "Poet's Corner" of Idi Amin's Uganda. *(slight pause)* After what seemed to be the longest five minutes of what remained of my life, they turned and drove towards Kampala. God save my two friends.

And grant me enough strength to come out of the marsh so at least my mother can see the body. It's so dark. The abduction was around nine. The latest it can be is eleven-thirty. By dawn, I will finally leave the world.

(to audience) I turned towards the east; a few metres in that direction was a foundation stone for a monument that was never built: "To the memory of all that had died in Idi Amin's Uganda."

He summons incredible energy and drags himself out of the marsh.

I stumbled eastward. Got to the road. Turned towards the highway. *(Pause. His inner voice takes over.)* Zigzag on the edge of the tarmac, George. Avoid leaving a blood trail.

He points to the other side after a few more steps.

(to himself) That's the spot where the shooting was. The sky is getting even darker. Around me, a misty grey colour. The pain throbs like unrelenting high-pitched drums. Tears are welling in my eyes. The earth feels like a rag slowly pulled away under my elephantine feet. *(Pause. To audience.)* Still, I "walked," supporting myself by leaning against a tree or holding onto a branch.

My entire family, relatives, friends, places too, were rolling over the screen of my mind. All their faces looked shocked. Lord let this government not last, at least let them not kill too many people.

Soft throbbing drums.

The images kept on rolling. My entire life… its landmarks, primary school… the best years. Short, intense.

(internal) God, if there is a way of coming back to this earth… make me a little bird, a spirit of the woods and custodian of Namanve Forest. I will always come back to my nest at sunset and sometimes disrupt the foul murders… enable the victims to escape.

You, my ancestors, all of you; from Kabaka Kalema, whose remains lie in Mende; Kakungulu and Mugujula, the two valiant warriors. My grandparents back in Masaka. My grandmother, Bulaliya Nakiwala, you who always danced agile as a duiker without ever touching a drink in your entire life. Yekoniya Zirabamuzale, you who lost your sight but never your wisdom and legendary charity. My stillborn brothers, you who never left the void, please pave my way and ease my transition.

(to himself) I see distant flares cut through the dark hide of night…

Thunder is heard.

A few drizzles are dropping on my body. It's raining.

(internal) This is a good resting place. The Ministry of Works labour camp is close, someone will see the body and Radio Katwe, the grapevine telegraph, will do the rest. I also have an uncle not too far from here; if he is home, he will save the body and deliver the news.

(to audience) The right arm is already swollen by more than half its normal size.

The trees and the undergrowth swirl at an incredible pace. Their shapes begin to change, taking on the threatening ones of the gnomic creatures and spirits that inhabit my folklore.

I have made my peace and put my borrowed time to good use. I'm a bird flapping my wings and gazing at the husk that was my body. Maybe I'll be like Christopher Okigbo, the Nigerian poet: they say he was sent back to earth after his death. Condemned to sing his lines eternally at a village well. To this day when the little children are sent to the well, they sometimes hear a pair of little birds singing:

Now let us sing tongue-tied
Without name or audience
And make harmony,
Among the branches.

I don't recall anything else.

> *The drums stop. More thunder and lightning. A tropical downpour is heard. It stops. It is dawn, and we can hear birds and other forest sounds. A determined tropical sun makes its way through the foliage.* GEORGE *opens his eyes. Slight pause.*

(to himself) Am I in heaven or hell? *(another pause)* It must have taken about five long, frightening minutes to come to terms with the discovery that I was still alive. That was far more shocking than the previous night's events. There was a long pregnant moment of silence. As if body and spirit were getting into sync. *(Pause. Very muffled agony.)* The pain is enormous. The earth is wet and soggy. I can hear occasional trucks in the distance... Obote has finally returned to power.

You know how much I love life, Lord. Why tantalize me with another glimpse of it? *(pause)* If I had my way, my request would be to live long enough to tell this tale. But even if I lived long enough just to see my mother, I wouldn't complain. But home is Jinja, and Jinja is almost fifty miles away. And between here and Kampala, the military roadblocks are manned by Obote's henchmen who will ask me to identify myself and explain my wounds.

Will the forest be my perpetual prison? Perhaps all I can do is sing like Nsimb'egwire, the little girl in the proverb.

> *Flute.*

Yes, I feel a certain kinship with her. Understand her in a way I have never done. Her voice is clear as a bell.

A female voice is heard singing the solitary lyrics.

FEMALE VOICE   *(singing) Ani oyo*
Ani oyo ayita
Ku mutunda…

GEORGE   *(picks up the story from where it stopped)* She was not ready to quit yet. Unknown to her, neither was her father, who had recently returned from the hunting expedition. Something told him not to believe anything her stepmother said. So he put a search party together.

One day they heard a familiar voice.

Singing continues.

FEMALE VOICE   *(singing) Ku mutunda*
Kuliko Nsimb'egwire
Nsimb'egwire
Muwala wa Mbaire.

GEORGE   She had finally been found. Half rotten and famished, they unearthed her and headed home. As for me, Obote has finally returned to power— *(interrupting himself)* Who's that? A little boy. Must be about twelve.

He beckons to the boy.

Tontya. Who sent you?

BOY   They sent me to see whether the village lost one of our own. Whenever we hear the bullets at night we come to check in the morning.

GEORGE   Go check across the road. My two friends might be there…. No. *(immense relief)* Thank God. Then please, go back and tell them I'm the only one.

(to audience) Soon they arrived. Headed by an elder, a chief of some sort.

(to the villagers) No, they took all my papers… but believe me, there is nothing sinister about this. *(pause)* Thank you. Thank you all so very much for the risk you're taking. The little boy should go ahead as a scout. At a sign from him simply dump my body by the side of the road; should the worst come to the worst… well, at least you will have done your best.

The villagers load their delicate cargo onto their backs. They walk for a while, unload without any incident.

	(to audience) As soon as we got to the village, I was placed on the floor of a tiny grey concrete store, right next to the highway. More and more people were milling around. No one had ever come out of Namanve alive. Then said the chief…
CHIEF	What would you like to do?
GEORGE	I have an uncle around here. His name is George Kakaire.
	(to audience) We wasted no time after his arrival. Kampala was so near and yet so far. Our best bet was Jinja. There, the roadblocks were fewer and except for the one at the Owen Falls Dam, they were almost entirely manned by Tanzanian troops.
	The first roadblock was Mukono. We stopped. We soon got to Lugazi. Mabira Forest. Bulumagi. We'd finally reached the roadblock at the Nile; the one stop we feared most. Will our story work? *(slight pause)* "He had an accident between here and the last roadblock. We've been referred to the next hospital."
SOLDIERS	*Pole sana! Mumuharakishe. ("How sad! Rush him.")*
GEORGE	*(to audience)* It worked. We had finally crossed the mighty Nile. The next stop was home.
	Mother had just come out of the bathtub when Uncle George walked in. Before he said anything she asked:
MOTHER	What brings you here so early… is he dead?
UNCLE	Not yet. No. Dress up. He's in the van. We have to get him to the hospital.
GEORGE	*(to audience.)* At first my sister Mary and mother just looked at me through the window. With tears streaming down my mother's face they edged closer. Finally, they lifted the blanket. There was a little relief. At least the chest and stomach seemed intact.
	At the hospital, it was as if all of our friends had conspired to be on duty at the same time.
	Looking at the X-rays.
FRIEND	You're lucky. Doesn't seem to be any bone injuries. Two bullets have to be dislodged. One from the right thigh, the other from the right arm.
GEORGE	*(to audience)* All along, there were no questions asked. Down in my warm and cosy bed, highly impressed, I looked up at the ceiling… tried to sum it all up for myself. *(There is a knock at the door.)* Dr. Walugembe walks in.
WALUGEMBE	*(very calmly)* The surgeon in charge is already pacing up and down… asking leading questions. I'm not saying it's true, but

given his political stripes, there is no guarantee that if he got wind of your story... he may not leave you on the table.

GEORGE   *(to audience)* He didn't have to say any more. Outside a different car was waiting and ready to go. Destination: twenty-eight miles away, in the famous town of Iganga.

My sister Mary got to work.

MARY   See this?

GEORGE   *(to audience)* It was the bullet in the right thigh.

MARY   You have to tell the doctors it's come out. Lest they start drilling and fishing for it where it's not. It also left another wound. Remind them about it.

GEORGE   *(to audience)* There was something else on my mind this afternoon. Anybody with bullet wounds had to have a certificate of some sort from the police before getting any treatment. Dr. Walugembe would vouch for us. For my part, all I had to do was remember a story we had gone through in the car. Inside the operating theatre the story is subjected to a severe test.

(to doctor) My name is James Nyende, Doctor. I was over-speeding along the Jinja-Kamuli highway... it all happened so quickly and it's entirely my fault. Before I knew it, I was passing a roadblock manned by our esteemed army. Realizing my mistake, I'm sure they never meant to kill. If you ask me, they were extremely kind... in the execution of their duty... so to speak.

DOCTOR   How can you say you hadn't anticipated the roadblock?

GEORGE   I don't live here. In fact... I am a student... at the University of Nairobi.

DOCTOR   *(literally pouncing on him)* You can't say Kamuli in one breath and Nairobi in the other.

GEORGE   *(to the doctors)* With due respect to all of you, there is a difference between the Hippocratic Oath and the Spanish Inquisition. My pain is unbearable. With the last ounce of my physical and psychic energy, I put it to you, sirs, with all my heart, that I made a mistake. There's none but me to blame. But please don't turn this operating theatre into an abattoir. If I had committed any crimes against the state... believe me, I would be more than happy to face a firing squad. I'll answer any other questions after the surgery.

DOCTOR   Count one, two, three.

GEORGE   *(to audience)* Late in the afternoon, the next day, I open my eyes for the first time. What's this? There is a drip hanging over my head. Here, behind a partial screen in an open hospital ward. Why does it look so familiar? Their positions as well: Mary, Mother, my grandmother...

But oh... the pain is a lot worse, unparalleled by anything I'd gone through before the operation.

> *Closes his eyes for a moment. There is a beat to mark the passage of time.*

They have begun to arrive. Soon this corner of the hospital ward will be full to the brim with relatives and friends, just like Grandmother's house at Rubaga. One of the first ones to arrive is my Auntie Gladys.

AUNTIE   You look too anemic, my son.

MOTHER   For some reason they refused to give him even a single drop of blood.

AUNTIE   *(angry and sad)* I'm not surprised.

> *Methodically, she circles around pointing to the wounds.*

Look. Look. Look at this...

> *Pulls* MOTHER *aside.*

Can I tell you something, my dear sister? Of all the years of training and practise both at Mulago and the hospitals in London, I have never seen the like! Did you have a good look at those sutures? God, I hate it when people put my Christianity to the test. They stitched our son up like a gunny bag. Only post-mortem surgeons do that. *(whispers)* It's for dead bodies.

GEORGE   *(to audience)* Uncle Paulo Kasekende was the next one to arrive. Right next to him was my great-uncle, good old Brother Stephen. Now in his sixties. Still far from frail.

I had no doubt in my mind he would gladly have traded places with me or any other victim in the family.

He reminded me of Mark Antony on seeing Caesar's body.

BRO. STEPHEN   *(Vents his spleen. Quoting Shakespeare. Flourish of trumpets is heard.)*
"Oh judgment, thou art fled to brutish beasts,
And men have lost their reason...
You blocks, you stones, you worse than senseless things!"

> *Removes his glasses. Pulls out a handkerchief.*

"Oh you hard hearts, you cruel men..."
These dogs. These shameless, godless... beasts.

Forgive me. *(pause)* You know Brother Andrew.... Yes, the Canadian. He goes to Nairobi from time to time. He's promised to help. Once your condition improves, he'll have to get you across the border, God willing.

GEORGE   *(to audience)* Two weeks later we celebrated a rather sunken-eyed but warm Christmas. We had moved to an anonymous little house, right next to the district prison in Iganga. Auntie Gladys headed the underground medical team that included my cousin Besi and a male nurse. Except for the right arm, all the other wounds were healing fast.

Now I could sit and stand. But I couldn't stand the bedpan any longer! *(tries walking)* By hook or crook, I had to get to the toilet.

He toddles his way across the stage.

I stood under the mid-afternoon Boxing Day sun, pleased as punch.

Halfway between the toilet and the stairs, I stopped. First I heard a sudden, curious sound, then right in front of me—a military Jeep! They've finally caught up with me. *(slight pause)* They will take my body but not my spirit. The door opens. Brother Stephen steps out.

BRO. STEPHEN   Sorry for the lack of warning. These are Tanzanian officers. I talked to their commander himself. Yes, he *(slight pause)* was a student of mine during my years in Tanzania, and he graciously offered to help. Go in and say goodbye. We'll say a little prayer, then leave as soon as your grandmother is ready to board.

GEORGE   *(to audience)* Soon I was having my last look at the mighty Nile. Then came Mukono, Namanve Forest, Bweyogerere. I thought about all those people that had rescued me. Uncle George, the pilot, the gentleman who offered his car and drove us the morning after. Forgive me, I would like to pay tribute to the so-called African extended family. *(drum roll)* Then and in the days that followed, the stream of relatives that poured in to reaffirm their love, support, and best wishes, uplifted my spirits, hope, faith, and accelerated the healing process. Their presence alone gave me something to live for. Forever they will always be etched in my memory.

Another drum roll.

We finally arrived in Kampala. I even had a glimpse of the famous Nile Mansions from my front seat. After the roundabout at Kibuye, we stop off to let Grandma off.

Now in her sixties, so tall and erect. The lines on her face more pronounced than ever before. But no amount of oppression will remove the inner dignity and proverbial wisdom of Semei Kakungulu's daughter and granddaughter of a noble king of Buganda.

GRANDMOTHER   You come from a line of brave and courageous people. I need not say much. You've seen it all. You know! Just one favour: when we die, even when you hear we are all dead and gone, I beseech you, never come back to the land of your ancestors. Let us pray for one another.

GEORGE   *(to audience)* We embraced again. Scared of attracting too much attention at this busy intersection, I get back into the vehicle nursing a lump in my throat. We drove towards Kisubi.

Photographs are taken. A new identity card is issued. For the first time I use the name Seremba, a name I had never used before, officially. I'm also listed as a postulant, a brother in the making, so to speak. The card also calls for a brand new story: I had gone to visit some friends in a senior seminary in Masaka diocese. All of a sudden the car swerved off the road. *(flashing a smile)* You should see the condition it's in! But God is great. If all goes well I should be back in two weeks. Just as soon as a few more experts examine me. God knows I love Uganda. *(a quick wink to the audience)*

Brother Andrew and Brother Aidan were both flying on the twenty-eighth. My name had been attached to their travel permit clearance form, signed and stamped by no less a man than the Honourable Minister for Internal Affairs.

The next afternoon, Dad came to say hello and goodbye. We shook hands. Embraced. Shook hands again. I knew, at least in his eyes, I was a hero.

That evening Auntie Gladys arrived. Offered me a sling for my right arm.

AUNTIE   You have now become a seasoned patient… from time to time you may have to dress the wounds yourself. I hope they get to look at that arm again soon. *(slight pause)* Son, always remember to thank God and the rain. Without that and your will, this would be a different story. So remember to get down on those knees. And don't forget to say "Come good rain, for there's none but I, to bear my cross."

GEORGE   *(to audience)* As we drove to the airport the next day it was Mother's turn to bid me goodbye.

MOTHER	God alone knows how many of us you'll ever meet, if things change. You know the rest as you have yourself witnessed. I beseech you though, do us one favour; please do not write this story. Wait.
GEORGE	*(to audience)* It is Sunday, December the 28th. Obote the "first and second" was sworn in last night. There is not much staff in the airport because of the big victory celebration the night before. Brother Stephen leaves us at the check-in counter and goes to the waving bay where Mary, Mom, and the rest are.
	Brother Andrew has already started chatting with some acquaintances. They let Brother Aidan pass. After a few casual explanations, I pass through too. With Brother Aidan at the front and Andrew at the back we proceed to board.
	Panting and nervous, he stumbles across the tarmac.
	Halfway up the stairs I take one last look.
	Inside the plane, a flight attendant's voice comes on.
FLIGHT ATTENDANT	*Mabibi na mabwana, tunawakaribisha ndani ya* Kenya Airways… *("Ladies and gentlemen, we welcome you on board Kenya Airways…")*
GEORGE	*(to audience)* We were up in the clouds.
	(Closes his eyes. Internal.) Thank you, Lord. Goodbye, Uganda.
	(to audience) Soon we would be getting into Kenyan airspace. Lake Victoria would be behind us, over the Rift Valley…. We finally landed at Jomo Kenyatta International Airport.
	It was my turn to go through customs and immigration.
OFFICER	*Wapi Kitambulisho?*
GEORGE	*(to audience)* I can't believe it! I go through all my pockets. Hand luggage. No sign of my identity card. Check again. Nothing!
OFFICER	You'll have to board the next flight back to Entebbe.
GEORGE	It must have dropped on my seat or the toilet.
OFFICER	This is a country, not a toilet. That plane is leaving for Mombasa. You'll have to go back to Entebbe.
GEORGE	Not with all these wounds…. Look, sir. *(points to one of the scars on the right leg then pulls his right sleeve and reveals a huge scar on the arm)* Besides, *niko mwalimu.* *("I am a teacher.")* Here in your country. *(beat)* Yes. Kilungu Day High School, in Ukambani, they call it Kwa Mwanza.

OFFICER	You're lucky. That is my home area. No immigration officer is allowed to do this. But because you teach our children I'll let you go, but next time... next...
GEORGE	*(to audience)* Next time. Hmm... when would that be?
	With my arm firmly in the sling, I limp through a corridor and behind a door for my first pee on Kenyan soil. *(brief pause)* Here is to freedom. That evening we knock on the door of the Rubadiri's at Hurlingham. *(to them)* Lazarus has come to see you.
	(to audience) The whole family gathers. All sure glad to see me. David, too, is short of words.
DAVID	My son, you are larger than life. Do you feel sorry for yourself, my son?
GEORGE	No.
DAVID	Here. This is more important than the medicines.
GEORGE	*(to audience)* David opens a bottle of brandy then places something on the turntable. A Welsh voice booms its way through the African night.
VOICE	"Do not go gentle into that good night, Old age should burn and rave at close of day; Rage, rage against the dying of the light."
GEORGE	*(to audience)* If there was rain that night, I didn't hear it. Two little birds stood guard against my window. Their sweet song cut my dream short. But I do remember seeing a stepmother hastily pack and desert her home after an abominable act, to live like a pariah for the rest of her life. Then I saw a beautiful young figure. Her song sounded familiar:

   He sings.

Abe mbuutu
N'abe ngalabi
Banange munkubire ngenda
Mbaire Yagenda nga alidda...

   GEORGE *relights and picks up the candle, and returns to the place on the stage where he first began. There is a slow fade to black. He blows out the candle and exits*

   The end.

George Bwanika Seremba was born in Kampala, Uganda. He started writing and acting at Makerere University, but it was during his years of exile in Kenya that he began to come into his own as an artist. Kenyan audiences remember him for his production of Athol Fugard's *Blood Knot* in which he performed the role of Zach. He would return to the same role a few years later at Prairie Theatre Exchange (Winnipeg) and at the Edmonton Fringe where his performance earned him even more accolades.

In Canada he has appeared in numerous productions, including *Our Country's Good* at Alberta Theatre Projects, *Separate Developments* at GCTC, *Majangwa* at the Manitoba Theatre Centre Warehouse, and *Master Harold and the Boys* at the Centaur Theatre (Montreal), the Citadel Theatre (Edmonton), and Theatre Passe Muraille (Toronto). He also starred in the 1990 feature film *The Midday Sun*, and has appeared in other movies, radio, and television series, including *Adderly* and *Counterstrike*. He also played Mr. M in his fourth Fugard, *My Children! My Africa!*, at the Studio Theatre (Harbourfront) and Theatre Aquarius in Hamilton.

In Ireland, while completing his Ph.D. thesis, *Robert Serumaga and the Golden Age of Uganda's Theatre* at the Samuel Beckett Centre for Drama and Theatre Studies (Trinity College, Dublin), he appeared in the critically acclaimed Calypso Production of *Master Harold and the Boys* in the role of Sam. George now has a doctorate and is trying to find a balance between his academic and creative pursuits as he contemplates a return to Toronto.

George is the author of three one-act plays, including his most recent one: *Mama's George* based on the short story *If George Could Speak* by Melatu Uche Okorie. His first full-length play, *The Grave Will Decide*, was written during his early years in Canada. He then wrote *Come Good Rain* and *Napoleon of the Nile*. An adaptation of *Come Good Rain* was aired on CBC Radio's *Vanishing Point* in May 1993. A radio version of his most recent full-length play, *Secrets of the Savannah*, was adapted and aired on RTE Radio, Ireland's national broadcaster, in 2007 as part of their Amnesty Season.

Je me souviens

Je me souviens was first produced by the Firehall Arts Centre, in co-production with Curious Tongue and Touchstone Theatre Company, Vancouver, British Columbia, in January 2000, with the following company:

LORENA	Lorena Gale

Director	John Cooper
Lighting design	Gerald King
Slide design	Tim Matheson
Sound design	John McCulloch
Choreography	Denise Lonewalker and Lorena Gale
Stage management	Diana Stewart Imbert

— • —

It was subsequently produced by the Belfry Theatre Company, in co-production with Curious Tongue in February 2000, with the same company.

— • —

Je me souviens was presented as a work-in-progress at On the Waterfront Festival by Eastern Front Theatre in Dartmouth, Nova Scotia, in May 1998 and at One Yellow Rabbit's High Performance Rodeo, Calgary, Alberta, in January 1999.

Characters

LORENA

JE ME SOUVIENS

Memories of an expatriate Anglophone,
Montréalaise, Québécoise, exiled in Canada

1

*Black. Music. Robert Charlebois's "Lindberg" bleeds into "This
Land is Your Land, This Land is My Land." The music ends with
the sound of a needle being scraped over a record. The lights
come up on a black stage with a large white projection screen
centred upstage. White material is arranged in gentle peaks
beneath the screeen and extending its length. Upstage is a
white chair. Projected onto the screen is a slide of Joe's Café in
Vancouver. We hear ambient café sounds in the background.
LORENA enters from the audience.*

LORENA   *(speaking directly to the audience)* I am on Commercial Drive,
sitting in Joe's Café. I'd just bumped into another expatriate and,
like those from the old country, hungry for news from home;
whenever we meet we always reminisce or share news of the others
we have left behind. It's a ritual of love and remembrance played
out on alien soil by émigrés all over the world. Only we're in
Vancouver and home is Montreal. The same country. At least
today it is.

She moves the chair to centre stage and sits.

We speak in English, my first language and her second. We
speak in English because I don't know Greek. We speak candidly,
without forethought, without apology. Around us we hear
snatches of Italian, Arabic, Spanish, Portuguese, Cantonese,
Urdu, et cetera. We speak unashamedly and to each other.

So I say to my compatriot, "I have just come back from Montreal.
I can't believe how much it's changed. Everything for sale.
Everything for rent. Liquidation. Going out of business. And
everywhere those tacky dollar stores. And they're the only ones
who seem to be doing any real business. It's sad. I have never seen
Montreal looking so bad."

And the next thing I know, there's this long-haired grunged-out
French guy in my face saying—

She stands.

—"Hey you! You don't say dat! You don't talk about Montréal!"

He had been listening in on our private conversation, which had obviously offended him, and had half-risen from his seat to stretch across his table and point an accusatory finger at me, like he was the long arm of the Language Police and had nabbed himself another Anglo traitor. He looked irate and triumphant like one spoiling for a fight. My friend immediately put her head down like somebody trying to avoid one. Me…? I was stunned into momentary silence.

What could I have possibly said to offend anyone? That Montreal looked poorly and depressed? The truth? For a second there I thought I was in a café on St. Denis Street, a little too drunk, voicing my insensitive Anglo opinions a little too loud, and this brave soldier in the struggle for Quebec independence was standing forth to eradicate this heretic from their midst.

I looked around expecting to see a room full of hostile and contemptuous people but no one was paying attention. I was still in Lotus Land. And what did I care since I wasn't talking to him anyway. So I told him to "fuck off and mind your own business!"

"Non! You fuck off! It is my business. Me. I'm from Montréal. You don't say nutting. Tu n'as pas le droit!"

I don't have the right? I don't have the right!?

My friend hates confrontation. She tells me to "…ignore him. He's an asshole. He's just looking for a fight. Come on. Let's go somewhere else."

But I have gone somewhere else. Thirty-six hundred miles to somewhere else. And I cannot back down.

"I don't have the right! Why? Because I'm English? Why? Because I'm Black!?"

"Ah, you. You don't know nutting."

"Oh! Je sais, moé. Je sais assez que toi, hostie. Et si je n'avais rien su, j'aurais eu le même droit de parler que toi!"

"Toi? Tu parles français!?"

"Oui. Je parle français. Je vien de Montréal, moé. Je suis Montréalaise. Je suis née a Montréal. Et j'ai le droit à parler. Le même droit à parler que toi, hostie! Avec n'importe qui, n'importe où—okay? So fuck off!"

"Eh, eh, eh! C'est correct. Je m'excuse. You come from Montréal. I t'ought…. You know, I from Montréal too, eh. And I t'ought…"

He picked up his backpack and wandered out onto the Drive. My friend was examining the residue at the bottom of her cappuccino. She hadn't said much through the entire altercation and I could tell she wanted to go, too. I still wanted to share my memories of Montreal. But the moment was lost. She had to run. And so we parted.

Slide—the rainbow mural on the exterior of Joe's Café.

You know, I'd see him on the Drive, from time to time, with a group of other young Québécois beneath the rainbow outside of Joe's Café. His shoulders hunched from the weight of his pack. His long hair matted into incongruous dreads. He is all passion and gesture and speaks French with a fury so familiar, but I can no longer follow. And when I pass he mumbles "salut" in grudging recognition.

We are both, after all, from the same place. His Montréal is my Montreal. His Québec is the Québec of my birth. Like heads and tails, we are two faces of the same coin. One side inscribed in French. The other English. And we are both so far from home.

I am an expatriate anglophone, Montrealaise, Québécoise, exiled in Canada. And I remember. Je me souviens…

2

Gilles Vigneault's "Mon Pays" begins playing. Lights fade out as footlights come up, projecting LORENA*'s shadow on the screen. The music fades into a dream-like sound, the soft whistling of wind.*

LORENA   Je me souviens d'un rêve que j'avais souvent… depuis mon enfance. Dans le rêve c'est l'hiver. Et je suis toute seule dans une plaine. Une grande plaine de neige. Y'a de la neige partout. Autant que les yeux peuvent voir. Pas d'arbres. Pas de maisons. Rien que la neige. De la neige qui n'a pas été defiguré. Immacule. Implacable. Pure.

Le soleil est un cercle parfait d'un jaune foncé; suspendu dans un ciel qui est bleu, bleu et clair. Et c'est froid. Tellement froid. Si froid… que ca pique. Et les rayons du soleil sur la neige… aveuglante. Je veux rentrer chez moi, mais je ne sais pas où je suis. Aucun signe de civilisation. Je suis perdue. Je suis perdue dans une plaine de neige aveuglante.

The footlights fade out.

3

LORENA

(*as* ETHEL, *a West Indian woman*) You know what de problem is wit you Canajun Blacks? You don't know where you come from. Ya don know who y'are. Ya talk like Whitey. Ya act all so-so like Whitey. Hell. You even move like you got a rod shoved up your arse to brain. All jig-jig like a puppet. And dat's de problem wit you. You let the White man into your head and now you all messed up. You don tink straight. You Black on de outside, White on the inside. You're assimilated. Assimilated Negroes. Dat's what you are.

Blackout. Text is projected onto the screen.

Slide—(text)
When people ask me which island I come from, I say Montreal. And they look confused.
When people tell me to go back where I came from—I look confused.

4

We hear the opening notes to the theme from Star Trek.

Slide—family photographs from Little Burgundy, an area of Montreal.

LORENA

(*impersonating* CAPTAIN KIRK) Captain's log. Star date nineteen-hundred and sixty-one.

We have been living among a small tribe of coloured outcasts in an area of the city known today as Little Burgundy—located within the outer perimeter of the downtown central core. Our crew, assembled from Jamaica, Sri Lanka, New Guinea, Bermuda, and St. Catharines, Ontario, have spent more than seventy-five earth years and three human generations in this location. But our work here has come to an end.

May 1st, 0800 hours. We leave downtown. Travelling at warp speed, east along Dorchester.

Slide—Dorchester Boulevard.

North on Park Avenue.

Slide—Park Avenue.

West on Bernard—

Slide—Bernard Street.

—and north again on Durocher.

Slide—Durocher Avenue.

Succesfully circumventing Mont Royal—the pimple local inhabitants call a mountain—in the middle of the city.

We have set a course for Outremont. Our mission—to seek life in new neighbourhoods. To boldly go where no Black has gone before!

LORENA *sings the* Star Trek *theme.*

5

We hear a soundscape of voices: English, French, Dutch, German, Italian, Hebrew, Yiddish, Arabic, and Russian. They are speaking in hushed whispers.

LORENA

French filters through as ambient sound, and English is spoken heavily and accented. Our new neighbours' names are Van Doorn, Petrovich, Leiberman, Mancini, Papanicalopolis, Osler, Azra. And each one speaks a language I cannot understand and sounds stranger to me than I look to them.

Men with *payos* and long dark coats and fur-rimmed hats, even in summer, huddle in the middle of the sidewalk passionately discussing the Torah in Yiddish. Greek mothers hang out their windows and holler for their kids, "Yanni, Stavros. *Ella thò.*" Italian men in cotton undershirts sit on kitchen chairs drinking wine out on the stoop and smack their kids for stealing a sip.

Did we really move across the city or to another continent?

"Immigrants," my mother calls them. "Beings from another country. Not born here like us."

But no one is like us in Outremont.

They say…

We hear the sound of "Go back where you came from" being spoken in different languages.

Slide—(text)
Go back to where you came from

But I cannot understand them.

6

LORENA

Mr. Camille lives next door. He is a friendly old man with watery eyes and splotchy red skin and sits on his balcony chain-smoking Players Plain and rocking back and forth. Sometimes he sends me

to Finast's to get his cigarettes. But I am not allowed to cross the
street. So I go up to Frank's, which is on the same side. And when
I get back he gives me a nickel! He tried to give me a dime once
but I gave it back. Nickels are better. They're bigger than dimes.

Mrs. Camille only wears cotton house dresses with faded floral
patterns and the same tan cardigan. Whenever you see her she has
a smile on her face but I know... she cries all the time. I know
because my bedroom wall is shared with theirs. I often hear her
muffled sobbing, moaning, sometimes wailing on the other side.
She tries to hide it but I can tell. Her eyes are as red as the smile
she paints on her face.

(as a child) Mr. Camille? Why does Mrs. Camille cry all the
time...?

(as MR. CAMILLE) My vife. She is not alvays so happy. But vhy
should you care. You are just a little girl. Vhy vould a little girl
vant to know such things. Vhat can I tell you than you vould
understand.

 Sits down.

Vhy does Mrs. Camille cry? How can I explain?

Do you know vhat is Holocaust? No. You are too young to know
this. Do you know what are Jews? Mrs. Camille and I, ve are Jews.
Jewish people. And ve are... different! Yes. Vherever ve go in
the vorld ve are different. Maybe not so much here. But ve are
different.

Some people in the vorld... they don't like different. Some people
in the vorld think they are so much better than everyone else. Not
because they do things that are extraordinary or good. No. They
just think they are better. And they vant everyone to be like them.
This, of course, is impossible. But this is vhat they vant. And if you
are not like them, if you are different.... Then they persecute you.
Try to control you. Enslave you. To kill you.

Ve Jews for many centuries were slaves. Yes, just like you and
your African people. Ve too were slaves vonce. But slavery is not
tolerated so vell anymore. So they persecuted us. Tried to kill us.
All of us. And this is vhat is the Holocaust. But some of us
escaped.

 Lifts up shirt sleeve and shows wrist.

See? Venever you see this you vill know it vas a Jew who escaped
death.

Mrs. Camille... she escaped too. But many, many millions did not
escape. Mrs. Camille's mother, Mrs. Camille's father, her sister Yeti,

her brother David. All vere lost in Holocaust. And that is vhy Mrs. Camille cries sometimes. She cries because she misses her family.

You are a smart girl, I think. Smart enough to ask qvestions. Yes. The answers maybe you don't like or understand so vell. But one day everything vill make sense to you. I vant you to remember vhat I'm telling you. Because you, too, are different. And it is important that you remember.

These people, who think they are so great. They are so superior. These people are everyvhere! Yes. These bad people are still all around us. Even here. In this Montreal. Today. That is vhy you and me must never forget who ve are. Because ve are different ve must remember. Because if ve forget, it could happen all over again. Do you understand?

> *Beat.*

Good. Now take your nickel and go buy some candy. I have had enough of your qvestions for one day. And don't ask Mrs. Camille. She doesn't like to talk about it. Go!

7

Music beings playing, "Sh-Boom."

LORENA   *(speaking directly to audience)* Outremont, Montreal, Quebec. The sixties. Before *Star Trek*. Before "Black Power." Before "Say it loud, I'm Black and I'm proud." Before "Black is beautiful." Black people were said to have hair like steel wool, liver lips, and some people even believed we had tails.

"Don't ever let a White man rub your head!" my mother warned. Like the fat polished tummy of a Buddha, they would rub your head for luck.

My mother cleans like one possessed and dresses me for Sunday every day. The whole flat sparkles with a maniacal gleam and I, too, am squeaky clean and proper. When she's not cleaning, she's working; cutting loose threads and sewing labels on children's clothes delivered in large boxes to the flat. Or studying into the wee hours for her nursing exam.

She says they think we are dirty and lazy. So we must always be careful how we present ourselves. We must always put our best foot forward and strive to excel excellence. Hard work and cleanliness are the key.

I don't know who "they" are. I don't care what "they" think. I want to play.

She sits.

Instead I sit like Atlas on the balcony and watch the other grubby children on the ground below rev imaginary engines in their Dinky cars, making roads in the dust.

(as LILLIAN*)* Don't be asking me to go down there. There is nothing on these streets for you. And I won't have you running around like some wild street urchin trying to find that out. Don't you know that's what they expect from us? You've got everything you need right here. So make yourself content.

Beat.

I know you think I'm being hard on you right now. But you have got to understand. We're coloured and we're living in the white man's world. Don't think for a moment that you can do like they do.

Lights to black.

8

Slide—(text)
HOW TO GET BY IN THE WHITE MAN'S WORLD.

LORENA   *(reading)* "How to get by in the White man's world."

"Jazzoid" music begins playing. LORENA *retrieves a pointer from under the white material, moves to beside the screen and reads from the slide.*

Slide—(text)

Don't talk back.
Don't raise your voice.
Don't wear loud colours.
Don't do anything to draw attention to yourself.
Smile even when it hurts.
Just try to fit in.
And don't rock the boat.
If anyone stops to speak to you, answer them politely and only if you have to.
Otherwise keep on moving.
Walk like you know where you're going.
Keep focused on what's ahead of you.
If you run into some commotion, don't stand around gawking.
Don't try to help.
Just keep on moving.
If it looks like trouble is coming towards you then cross the street.

If it looks like trouble is sneaking up behind you then run.
If you're surrounded, then fight.
Keep your eyes and your ears open at all times.
If you find yourself in a situation—don't go to a policeman and don't stand still.
Just keep on moving and you'll be safe.

> LORENA *puts the pointer back under the white material.*

9

Slide—(text)
HE WHO FIGHTS AND RUNS AWAY, LIVES TO FIGHT ANOTHER DAY.

"Nigger" is being whispered harshly in different languages.

LORENA Outremont, Montreal, Quebec, Canada. We are called "nigger" in two official languages, as well as several unofficial ones. "Black," too, is a fighting word. But sounds like "Negro" in so many languages, I do not respond. My brother's fists fly daily.

It is the English slur that is the slur of choice. Even with French kids, who find that "negresse noire" does not have the right rhythmic impact. Anglo-, franco-, and allophone children walk in packs behind you, chanting: "niggerblack, niggerblack, niggerblack," on the way to school. All the way to school. I walk alone.

10

A loud school bell rings.

Slide—the Union Jack.

LORENA *(as a child)* I pledge allegiance to this flag and to the Commonwealth for which it stands. *(singing)* God shave our gracious queen. Shave her with shaving cream. God shave the queen. Send her to Halifax. Make her pay all the tax…

(as MISS BENNETT, an English grade-school teacher) Enough. Good morning class.

(as a child, fidgeting) Good morning, Miss Bennett.

(as MISS BENNETT) Open your geography books to page thirty-seven. Chapter six. Bunga of the Jungle.

> *She snaps her fingers and the lights go out.*

> *Slide—a turn-of-the-century depiction of a tribal Africa.*

Bunga of the Jungle. The jungle is a rain forest located in the Belgian Congo. The heart of deepest, darkest Africa. Can anybody tell us about Africa? Lorena?

Silence.

Bunga is an African. Africans are little primitive peoples with black skin—Lorena. And tight woolly hair—Lorena. And broad flat noses, who run about the jungle naked, climbing trees for fruit, digging in the earth with crudely shaped tools for tubers and nuts, and killing elephants—

Slide—a nineteenth-century photograph of African hunters surrounding a dead elephant.

—with poison darts they blow through long tubes. Well...

Chuckles and pats LORENA'*s chair.*

Maybe not you. *(beat)* While we're on the subject...

Snaps her fingers and the lights come up.

There are many starving children in Africa. As you can imagine, they don't have lots of good things to eat like we have here. They don't have milk to drink, or mashed potatoes, or grilled cheese sandwiches on Wonderbread. They sleep right on the floor in houses made of straw—they don't even have any walls—and drink out of the same watering holes with the zebras and crocodiles. Well. These poor children obviously need our help.

She takes an orange UNICEF *box from under the white material.*

That's why every year the good people at UNICEF ask nice Canadian children, like yourselves, to take this little box with them on Halloween and collect donations along with their trick-or-treats. The money you raise will be used to buy food, water, building materials, and even a few school books for all the poor hungry people in Africa. So, don't forget to pick up your UNICEF box before you leave the school. In fact, I'll just leave one right here on Lorena's desk. A helpful reminder.

Now, where was I...

11

The end of "Soul Man" fades into ambient party sounds.

Slides—photos of people listening to music and of parties are shown throughout the scene.

LORENA	There are voices in the night. Dark voices. Warm as gingerbread and comfortingly familiar. It's Saturday night and the folks have come up from downtown. My uncles, my sister's school friends.

The sound of "Groovin' (On a Sunday Afternoon)" by The Young Rascals fades in.

And they've bought chicken from the Chalet Lucerne. I can smell it, sweet and pungent, through the stench of cigarette smoke. And in the morning there will be a wing, my favourite part, saved for me.

Listening.

The Young Rascals croon softly in the background "Groovin'… on a Sunday Afternoon…"

A male voice rises. A murmured female reply. Then the multi-pleasured laughter of a mellowed crowd's response. Something groooovy is going on and I want to be a part of it.

LORENA sneaks toward the screen.

Slide—image of a large door, slightly ajar.

VOICE-OVER	A coloured man walks into a greasy spoon and sits at the lunch counter.

The waitress comes over and says, "Sorry, we don't serve niggers here."

The coloured man says, "That's all right. I don't eat them."

LORENA	Laughter explodes like a raisin in the sun, rising beyond humour to an almost hysterical crescendo. Then diminishes into painful recognition. Followed by silence. Interminable and dense. And when they speak again, their tones are hushed and sober.

(as a child, listening at the door) There's a man with a dream… and a woman on the bus… and a young boy hanging from a tree… the Panthers have left the jungle and have moved to the city… 'cause there's a war overseas… and coloured people are supposed to be free! They say the days of slavery are over… but the men in white hoods snatch you at night! That's why Chicago's burning… people are sitting in Arkansas. People are sitting in Alabama. Malcolm. No, Martin. No, Martin. No, Malcolm. No, Martin is going to overcome.

Slide—(text flashes onto the screen, superimposed on the image of the door, getting larger and larger each time, repeatedly through the scene)
Change.

VOICE-OVER	*(female)* When are we all going to be free?

	Slide—(text) Change.
LORENA	*(as a child, frightened)* Change.
VOICE-OVER	*(male)* I remember when they wouldn't serve us in the restaurants on St. Catherine Street. Or let us in the movie theatres…
LORENA	Change.
VOICE-OVER	*(female)* We have our rights.
	Slide—(text) Change.
LORENA	Change.
VOICE-OVER	*(female)* Education is the key.
	Slide—(text) Change.
LORENA	Change.
VOICE-OVER	*(male)* By any means necessary.
	Slide—(text) Change.
LORENA	Change.
VOICE-OVER	*(female)* Yet lift me up!
	(male) Hey. We could be doing a lot worse. We could be living in the States. Or South Africa with that apartheid shit. I'd say we're damned lucky to be Canadians.
	(female) When was the last time you tried to get out of downtown?
	(female) Oh, that doesn't mean anything. We have the laws to protect us.
	(male) Yeah. At least we don't have to worry about crosses burning and getting lynched.
	(female) Amen.
	(male) But folks are dying in America. For our rights.
LORENA	*(as a child, yawning)* The debate rages into the night. I fall asleep with my ear to the door.

12

In the black we hear bagpipes, feedback. The sound of a voice on a public address system.

ANNOUNCER   *(voice-over)* Guy Drummond Elementary School proudly presents… Multicultural Day!

Lights come up.

From Scotland...

LORENA does a Highland fling, smiles, and bows.

From Israel…

LORENA dances the hora, smiles, and bows.

From Greece…

LORENA dances to "Zorba the Greek," smiles, and bows.

From China…

LORENA picks up the mask of a dragon. Moves it around delicately, smiles and bows.

LORENA   *(as a child)* Look, Ma! I fit!

13

Lights change. We hear eerie-sounding music.

LORENA   A gang of kids waited for me in the schoolyard. "What will you do, now that your leader is dead?" they rumbled.

I ran home in fear of what they might do to me and found my mother slumped over the kitchen table, crying.

(as LILLIAN) They shot him. The bastards shot him. They couldn't let an intelligent Black man live. They couldn't lynch him, so they shot him. They shot him. Martin Luther King. They shot him dead on the ground.

Slide—photo of the assassination of Martin Luther King, Jr., in which people are pointing from their balconies in horror.

Oh, God! Our leader is dead, and my mother is moaning. I want to stop her tears, bring him back to life, anything to keep my mother's strength from crumbling before me. But she wasn't crumbling. She was angry and the fierceness she had always kept hidden from me was like fire in her eyes.

(as LILLIAN) Don't you ever trust the Whites. Don't you ever trust them. Every time you try to rise up, they'll beat you down again. They'll try to rob you of your dignity. They'll try to steal your

pride. They'll take everything you have in this world just to keep you in your place. They'll even take your life. But there is one thing God gave you that's yours to keep forever, and they can't take that from you unless you give it up to them. I'm talking about your soul, Lorena. Don't ever give away your soul. You hear me? I'm talking about survival in the white man's world.

Don't let them break your spirit. Don't ever let them break you. If they knock you down, get up again. If they try to hold you back, just keep on pushing forward. Don't take no for an answer. Don't give up, no matter how hard it gets. Just keep on pounding on that door and some day it will open for you. Keep reaching for the stars and you'll have the universe.

We are coloured. And though your race will seem like a weight around your shoulders, don't let anybody tell you that you aren't beautiful and good. You are the future. You have a right to the future. Don't let anyone take that away from you.

There was conviction in her voice and determination in the lines of her face. The dream that was Martin, the light on the periphery of my existence, flares in the heavens like a star turned nova and shines on me from my mother's eyes. They may have killed our leader, but they haven't killed our hope.

14

Bright white lights facing the audience flash blindingly—a whiteout.

Blackout.

Footlights come up, projecting LORENA's shadow on the screen. The music fades into a dream-like sound, the soft whistling of wind.

LORENA   …Je suis perdue dans un plaine de neige aveuglante. Je me couvre les yeux des mains, pour les protéger du soleil. Je regarde autour de moi. J'ai besoin d'un repère pour me diriger. Mais tout que je vois c'est le bleu et le blanc du ciel et de la neige.

Je commence à croire que je vais mourir là. Mon coeur et mon corps—complètement congelés. Je vais être retrouvé là, ou je me tiens, dans cette posture, comme une sculpture en glace solitaire, exposé dramatiquement sur un couche de neige.

Non. Je ne veux pas mourir comme ça. Il faut que je trouve un moyen de sortir d'ici. Il faut que je bouge.

Footlights fade to black.

15

We hear Aretha Franklin singing "I need love, love, love." LORENA
sings along.

Slide—photo of LORENA *as a teenager.*

Slide—(text superimposed on the photo of LORENA*)*
Oh Mama. Is anyone ever going to love me?

LORENA   Oh Mama. Is anyone ever going to love me?

(as LILLIAN*)* There's plenty of time for that nonsense! You've got
more important things to think about, like how you're going to get
by in this world. If you spent more time worrying about your
future than boys you might find yourself getting someplace. And
don't mess up your life by getting pregnant. Keep your skirt down
and your legs crossed and stay away from white boys!

16

Slide—(text)
5 REASONS TO STAY AWAY FROM WHITE BOYS.

Jazz music. LORENA *crosses to the screen and reads the following
slides aloud.*

LORENA   1. They only want one thing.
2. They don't commit to Black girls.
3. They think all Black women are whores.
4. They make promises they can't keep.
5. They won't respect you.

But there are no Black ones.

17

Slide—(text)
Amour.

LORENA   He says he loves me but he won't speak English. He says "Je t'aime,
Loren. Je t'aime." I want to believe him. But my name is Lorena.

He says he loves me but he won't speak English. He's a vrai Péquist
and won't dare to speak a word of the language of his oppressor.
But the truth is that my broken French is better than his English
and I think it embarrasses him.

When we're with his friends, he speaks a rapid-fire joual that's
bewildering to follow. I try to nod my head and laugh in the
appropriate spaces. But no one is fooled. Each exchange is

followed with "Comprends-tu?" Or explained in baby syllables, "Il-a-dit-que-blah, blah, blah. Comprends-tu?" And sometimes when I try to contribute to the conversation, I'm told to "just speak English." They say, "Tu parles français comme une vache espanol."

But when we are alone, his breath hot upon my neck, he murmers "J'aurais toujours envie de te serer fort dans me bras." I hear, "I will always want that you claw hard in my arms…!?" His words of love get lost in my kinky translations. Instead, I interpret the intimacy of his touch, the soft intensity in his eyes and abandon myself to the rhythms of his romantic language. I'm making love in French!

Then I understand that he will always want to hold me in his arms, because that is where I want to always be.

He says he loves me but he won't speak English. I turn to say "I love you too." But check myself and say "Je t'aime." I want to say more but the words get scrambled in my mind. Les mots ne viens pas facilement.

Slide—(text)
Si tu veut parler en français il faut que tu penses en français.

He says he loves me but he won't speak English. He wants to take me home! À Drummondville. Son endroit! I don't really want to go. My love life is like the lyrics of a Janis Ian song. I know what heartache lives along that road. Still we wind our way east along the St. Lawrence, through small towns with church spires gleaming white against a clear blue sky, meandering towards his history. The farther from Montreal we travel the more conspicuous I feel. I see surprise in the faces of diners in the Casse Croute in Saint-Hyacinthe where we stop for lunch. Some sneak a peak at me between bites of hamburger steak and others gawk openly like I'm some strange and shameful beast. He is oblivious to my discomfort. Love is blind.

Traditional Québécois folk music begins playing.

His folks are of vielle souche, les inhabitants, sturdy, unpretentious folk. Their faces warm and open. Omer, with belt buckle lost beneath his "grosse bédune" pumps my hand enthusiastically, "Bienvenue, bienvenue!" And Henriette, with her plain tan sweater buttoned devoutly to her neck, takes my face in both her hands and presses her lips to my cheeks. "Nous sommes très content de te voir. Enfin. Marcel avais parlé beaucoup de toi. Vienne. Vienne t'assoire. Une place speciale pour toi."

"Henriette don't speak no Henglish. Me. I don't speak good Henglish but I try."

"Comme vous voulez. Je parle français. Pas très bien, mais j'essaye aussi."

And we laugh.

I'm surprised. They want me to like them as much as I want them to like me.

 Slide—(text)
 Si tu veut penser en français, il faut que tu vives en français.

He says he loves me but he won't speak English. Big fucking deal! I am elated. He says he loves me and wants to live with me!

My Anglo friends complain they never see me any more. They feel betrayed. But they don't understand!

This language that I live in, this English I take shit for each time I leave home, is not my English! Each word's a link, each phrase a chain that's forged in centuries of slavery. I speak Massa's tongue. And though I've mastered the language of my subjugation, I still yearn for the authentic voices of the lost generations of my ancestry. We share in spirit a desire to preserve what's left of our shattered identities. Side by side we'll fight the powers of oppression and live as revolutionaries in the struggle for social change. Together we will smash the shackles of colonial domination. Two niggers in America united by love. Free at last. Free at last. Vive Québec libre! Free at last!

So I renounce my Anglo roots and move with him into a four-room flat on Colonial and Duluth.

We do the things that lovers do. Play in bed until two. Then crawl out into the afternoon sun, still entwined like differing plants that grow together, their leaves a tangle of familiarity. Inseparable. Window-shop on St. Denis and browse in bookstores along the way.

This book is far from ostentatious. No bold print or glossy cover screaming for a sale. But sepia-toned and made to look like aged and faded paper. It is the doleful Black face on the cover that rouses my curiosity and compels me to innocently pick it up and crack its spine.

They say a picture's worth a thousand words in any language.

 Faint Southern gospel singing is heard in the background.

It's not the smouldering remains of what had been a man that shocks me. His once-Black features charred beyond recognition.

It is the twenty or thirty white men that stand behind the pyre, proudly arranged like graduates for a picture.

> *Slides—different close-ups of the faces of respectable-looking white men in the crowd.*

Their triumphant smiles. Their self-satisfied demeanour. Their total unconcern for the life they took, for that life was of no value to them except in macabre sport. Their shameless hatred. They didn't even bother to wear their hoods or robes.

Exposed and smiling for the camera, their eyes all seem to follow me. Pandora's book! I want to snap it shut but it's too late. I've been identified.

He says, "Don't look. Loren. Don't look."

But I can't look away. I can't just look away.

> *Slides stop.*

He says he loves me. Even in English sometimes. His sudden fluency surprises me. But it really doesn't matter what language he says it in. Each time we pass that bookstore I have to stop and look.

Each time he says, "Don't look, Loren. Don't look. Why do you 'ave to look at that?"

These men, these men who think they are so great, they are so much better, these men are everywhere! I have to remember their faces. I forget sometimes who I am and where I ultimately come from. These men remind me that a lapse of memory could one day prove fatal. And I want him to look with me. It is important that he look with me.

Regard, Marcel. Regard. Quelle sort des hommes peuvent faire ça!?

> *Slide—the entire photograph of the respectable-looking white men is revealed. The crowd surrounds the charred remains of a lynched Black man.*

He says he loves me. He says "I love you, Loren. I look at you and I see you. I don't see no colour. Just Loren. And I love him. Her."

I want to believe him. But I am more than the languages I speak. Who I am is embedded in every cell of my skin. How can he love what he can't see? What he won't see?

18

We hear hot, restrained jazz; Dexter Gordon's "Tanya."

Slide—(text)

THE DISCOVERY OF WHAT IT MEANS TO BE A CANADIAN.

Slides—photos of the city at night, and angry, intense, and despairing faces of Black people throughout the scene.

LORENA I was blind but now I see. I see it everywhere. In the eyes of the "other" that seem to look right through me as if I am not there. In the eyes of the dark and dispossessed, red-rimmed with watery rage suppressed and masked with stoicism.

I see what my mother strove so hard to spare me, prepare me for: a world that's quick to judge a person solely on the basis of the colour of their skin and not on their merit. A world where white is might and if you happen to be born Black—well, there's always room at the back of the bus otherwise, step down.

And this world isn't south of anywhere. It's north. True north. Strong and free. But only for the fair.

I walk…

Slide—(text)

TO BE BLACK AND ENLIGHTENED IN TODAY'S SOCIETY IS TO BE IN A CONSTANT STATE OF RAGE.

…unemployed and almost homeless. Through streets of slushy grey, raining grey rain from a grey sky. Relying on the kindness of strangers and finding most are all too familiar in their response.

I see—

LORENA claps her hands and turns her head as if slapped in the face.

—why each apartment's just been rented when I show up for a viewing! I see—

Claps again and reacts as if slapped.

—why the perfect candidate just precedes me at each job interview! Is it my stomach rumbling? Or the awakening anger within?

I walk…

Like a target through these streets.

Past scores of Haitian cabbies, fired from the SOS Cab Company for being what they cannot change.

Past three middle-aged Black women on their way home from church, being frisked by the police because they are suspect, suspected of being…

Past Anthony Griffin, gunned down by the authorities and lying in a pool of his own innocence and blood.

There's Ruben Francois,
Black Snow Goat,
waiting on the corner of Crescent and St. Catherines
with a can of gasoline in one hand
and a book of his self-published poems in the other.
There's a fire in his heart
though his smile is serene.
Anointing himself like a Buddhist priest,
he calls to me…

(*as RUBEN*) When the weight of life is on your shoulder,
Sister, don't show any sadness on your face
for no one will pity you. Oh, look at me now!

He calls to me…

(*as RUBEN*) Get up and fight!
It's everybody's everything!
He calls to me…

(*as RUBEN*) By god, I light the candle, burn the incense
the smoke in my head, a hole in my soul
proudly, walk I the streets in my search to be free
the spirit by my side, someday soon
you will know what I mean!

He calls.
Then sets himself ablaze in protest.

And I walk…
Past "white only" restaurants,
and "white only" taxi stands,
and "white only" apartment buildings,
and "white only" nightclubs
and I see the unlegislated signs of segregation.
Subtle and tacitly agreed upon.
Unspoken
in two official languages.

> *Slides—photos of Malcolm X and Martin Luther King, Jr. flash through images of fire. LORENA sits upstage with her back to the audience for about a minute while the music plays out.*

19

LORENA   (*as* ETHEL) I am tired, Lo. So tired of all dis French/English bullshit! Day in, day out. Dey threaten to close the hospital, you know? Notice is only the English one dey threaten. Dey layin' off people left and right. I lucky I still got me job. But I puttin' in double shift every other day. Some days me so tired I just see white.

But I ain't complainin'. I take every hour dey see fit to give me. I savin' my pennies. Because I know for you and me is not about French or English.

Here's what happened. I just finished putting in a double shift: eleven to seven, seven to three. All I want to do is go home and curl up in me bed, but I got to take de boy to de dentist. So I rush like hell from de hospital, grab de boy from his school, and race clip-clip to de dentist's office.

Now, I don't recognize de receptionist. But I don't pay it no mind. Dey change dese girls sometimes more often than dey change dheir undershorts. Dis one, skinny black-haired thing. She on de phone talking away and we standing dhere. We wait and we wait. Five minutes pass and we still standing dhere.

Finally she looks up at me and say, "What you want?"

I say, "We have an appointment at 3:30. Sorry we're a bit late."

She say, "That's impossible."

I say, "What you mean I don't have an appointment. My name is Ethel Martin. It could be under my son's name, Rasheed."

She say, "No. You have no appointment here."

Now me tinkin' what de hell's going on here? I take de appointment slip out of me pocket. I say, "But see. It says 3:30. Monday. The twenty-seventh."

She say, "I told you. That's not here."

You know dhese office buildings everyting looks de same? De same white reception counter, de same orange chairs in de waitin' area. De same damn pictures of happy teeth on de walls. Noting but dis bitch to tell me is different. I was on de wrong floor. How was I to know dhere was another dentist office directly below my own? I suppose I could have looked at de name on de door but I didn't. I was tired and in a hurry. It was a mistake. An honest mistake. Anyone could have made it.

So, me and de boy go leave and under her breath she says, "Stupid."

I don't know why I didn't let it slide. But I stop and turn around to her and I say, "You know. You are very rude."

And she come out from behind de counter, all red face, shouting, "You Black bitch! You get out of here!" And she shoves me through de doorway!

Now me feet ain't caught up wit' me body. I still got one in de office. She slam de door on my foot so hard de glass panel crack. And if dhat was not enough of an assault on my person, she follows me into de hall with her "stupid dis" and "Black dat" and "go back where you came from" and hitting on me and pushing me around.

I look at me boy. His eyes wide and shiny. I never seen him look so scared. He's moving back and forth like so. He's saying, "Mommy, Mommy, let's go, Mommy." But dis crazy bitch won't let me go. And then she turn and raise her hand to strike my child. Well, I just pulled back me fist and popped her one in de face! Grabbed de boy's hand and went on about my business.

After his appointment, we step out of de building and dhat bitch is dhere wit' de police.

"C'est elle!" she yells. And de next ting I know, I am being arrested for assault. Dey handcuff me hands behind me back like I'm some dangerous criminal. Rummage through me handbag. Feel me up and down, so, like I got some deadly weapon up underneath me uniform. Right dhere on de street! And dey shove me and de boy in de back seat of de police car and take us to de station. All dat. All dat humiliation and degredation. Right in front of me child's eyes!

I don't go to court for a few months yet. You know dey wanting me to pay for de replacement of de glass panel dat bitch crack on me foot! De lawyer ain't worried. Plenty people waiting in the office. Good people willing to testify on my behalf.

But I tell you something. When dis nightmare is over, I am packing up me things and taking me boy to Toronto. How can I teach him to have respect for people who have no respect for him? If it's like dis now, what it goin' to be like when dey got dey own country, huh? I am forty-five years old. Ain't noting worth living out de rest of my life like shit on the sole of a Frenchman's shoe.

You damn right. I'm getting the hell out of here!

Whiteout.

20

Footlights come up, projecting LORENA*'s shadow on the screen.*

LORENA   Il faut que je trouve un moyen de sortir d'ici. Il faut que je bouge.

Au loin, très loin, il a quelques chose à peine perceptible. Un tout petit point noir ou le ciel et la neige s'embrassent à l'horizon.

Un tronc d'arbre peut-être. Une roche.

Pas à pas, je marche vers ce point. Mes yeux baissé, une tête basse contre les rayons de soleil. Je marche… pas d'empreinte dans la neige! Lentement, mais avec détermination. Il me semble que plus je marche, plus loin est la destination. Que je ne vais jamais y arriver. Mais c'est du mouvement et ca me réchauffe et je retrouve mon espoir.

21

Slide—photo of LILLIAN, *her hands covering her face.*

Slide—(text, beginning small and growing larger throughout the scene, flashing across the image of LILLIAN*)*
Go…

VOICE-OVER   Go…

LORENA   We are sitting on her balcony at the Rockhill Apartments. The sun rolls down the slopes of Mont Royal cemetery and dances off the crystalline patches of melting snow, tender green shoots of new spring grass, and the glistening headstones of the gone but not forgotten.

Bundled like a baby in Hudson's Bay blankets, she complains about the cold and dampness. Despite her discomfort, I insist that we stay outside for a little while longer. She rarely leaves the apartment anymore and needs the fresh air.

Slide—(text)
Go…

VOICE-OVER   Go…

LORENA   You would not know that she is fifty-seven to look at her. She still looks like she could be my sister and I am the youngest of her five adult children. It is her hands that reveal her internal age, which is about seventy-five. Her clothes disguise the rest.

Slide—(text)
Go…

VOICE-OVER   Go…

LORENA   These hands…. These hands have large misshapen knuckles and
                fingers that are crippled, bending at the joints every which way.
                Her "zeds" she calls them in an attempt at humour. But mostly she
                tries to keep them hidden from view.

                Slide—(text)
                Go…

VOICE-OVER   Go…

                LORENA rests her head on the chair.

LORENA   I drop to my knees and rest my head in her lap. And despite the
                pain I know she feels, she takes one of these hands and smoothes
                back my hair, caresses my brow.

                I say, "Oh Mama, is anybody ever gonna love me?"

                She says, "I love you."

                I say, "Oh Maw. That's not what I mean…"

                "You have plenty of time for that nonsense," she says.

                "But you've been saying that to me since I was fourteen years old."

                She takes a lock of my hair in her crooked fingers and tickles my
                ear, like when I was a child and she wanted to wake me. But I am
                awake and a woman now.

                Slide—(text)
                Go…

VOICE-OVER   Go…

LORENA   I say, "I've been thinking, Maw. What if that person that's meant
                for only me isn't in Montreal? Lord knows I've worn my heart out
                searching the city for them. What if they are somewhere else in the
                world? Just waiting to meet me. It's possible…"

                "Anything is possible," she says, "If you believe."

                And one of those hands attempts to squeeze my shoulder
                reassuringly.

                I say, as conversationally as possible, "You know Lisa's gone to
                Vancouver."

                She says, "Uh huh…"

                I say, "Yeah. Louise is in Ottawa. And Brenda just got this great job
                in Toronto. Pretty soon I won't have any friends left here at all."

                "Have you found a job yet?" she asks.

                "No," I say, "but I'm okay for a few months. Something will
                happen soon."

And for the longest time these hands sit silent and heavy on my shoulders…

"Go," she says. "Go to the farthest place. And work your way back. If you have to. You can always come back if you have to."

But how, in good conscience, can I leave these hands? These hands that slapped and nursed me? That played the "Moonlight Sonata" and delighted in braiding my hair? These hands can no longer carry a Steinberg's bag, button a blouse, pick a dime from a change purse, or brush her still-black and lustrous hair. These hands. How can I leave these aching hands? How can I leave these hands when they obviously need me so?

As if reading my thoughts she adds, "As long as I am here you will always have a home to come back to. So go. Go. Don't worry about me. I'll be just fine. I have survived this long, haven't I?"

I put my arms around her waist and bury my face in her lap. The osteoarthritis is all through her body and though it pains her to be held, she endures my embrace. I smell her through the blankets. The smell beneath her perfume. Her smell. I love her smell. How can I leave her smell?

She pats me on the back and laughs, "I'll help you pack."

And then these hands release me, like a thousand yellow butterflies fluttering goodbye.

> LORENA, *kneeling by the chair, waves goodbye.*

22

> *The sound of an airplane.* LORENA *retrieves a black and white umbrella from under the white material. She raises the umbrella.*

> *Slides—rainy Vancouver scenes and people with umbrellas.*

LORENA   Rainrain rain rain rainrain rain rain rain rain rain rainrain…

Dear Louise,

Greetings from soggy Vancouver! It has been raining for eight days straight and the streets are covered in slugs. Brown slimy things, not unlike long runny turds that ooze along the sidewalk. The streets are just slithering with them. Really gross.

I can't believe it's been three months already. It feels like for-fucking-ever.

I have moved out of my sister's windowless basement in Surrey, into a one-bedroom apartment in the downtown west end. There's nothing in it except my bed. But it's three blocks from English Bay, and I have developed a fondness for sitting on the beach and "watching the ships roll in"—just like in that Otis Redding song. Yes, girl, Lorena on the beach! I'm doing nature! (You can't avoid it out here. It's fuckin' everywhere!) Mind you, I am going to have to get appropriate footwear. My heels keep getting stuck in the sand.

I got myself a little job at an all-night depanneur, excuse me, convenience store about four blocks from where I live. I had a job in market research, but I got fired when I didn't show on June twenty-fourth. I said, "Hey, it's St. Jean Baptiste Day. A holiday!" They said, "Not here it ain't." And gave me the boot! It's just as well. I was getting tired calling people and asking them intimate questions about their feminine protection.

So how's life in Ottawa? Capitol punishment? I don't know about you but I am finding it hard adjusting to life in Canada. First of all, people don't know how to dress here. Everyone looks like they just crawled out of a kayak or some other outdoorsy thing. Bush bunnies. They wear big cloddy boots all the time. (The better to stomp slugs with I guess.) I find I am overdressed for just about every occasion. And I can't even dress properly because there's not one place in the whole fucking city that sells flesh-coloured pantyhose the colour of my flesh!

I won't even talk about makeup or hair products.

There are no Black people in Vancouver. I can go for days where the only Black face I see is my reflecion in a store window. And when I do see another Black person, I stop and try to flag them down.

Everything closes down at one A.M. like some fucking temperance colony. You can buy pornography at the corner store but not beer and wine. (Figure that one.) And people get in your face for just about everything; for smoking cigarettes, for swearing, for waving your hands and raising your voice when you get excited. Don't get passionate and above all, don't get political. It's like there is some law against having a good time here. The BC No Fun Laws. They are really frustrating.

And English! It's so omnipresent. Did you know that the STOP signs actually say STOP!? In big bold white letters!? And nothing else!? Is it like that everywhere in Canada? Everywhere, unilingual English signs. It's creepy.

And I don't understand this English. Back home, you were Italian, you were Greek, Polish, Hungarian, Dahomian, whatever, you spoke English, it was an agreement. A way of establishing common bonds. You were a part of something. It made you feel like a revolutionary. But here, they use it to bludgeon people with. Particularly immigrants. They say, "You're in Canada now. Speak English!" And there is actually a group called the "Society for the Preservation of the English Language and Literature." It's probably just a bunch of old Brits sitting around eating mushy peas and singing "Rule, Britannia!" But still, it's offensive. I feel like I just traded one kind of language prejudice for another.

I got a call from Peter. He's thinking of moving out here. And do you remember Leslie? She lives just two apartments down from me. I keep running into all kinds of folks from home. Every day there's a new batch of refugees—French and English. It's funny, in Montreal none of us would give each other the time of day but here… we cling to each other. There's a gang of about twenty of us expatriates. We get together every so often to eat and drink and smoke and talk and swear real loud. Hell, we even speak French and we don't have to, anymore. We go to restaurants that promise a taste of home—Montreal-style bagels and Montreal-style smoked meat and Montreal-style barbecued chicken. We have come to the conclusion that there's a pokey little town somewhere in Missouri named Montreal, 'cause we ain't et anything in Montreal, Quebec, that tastes this shitty.

The one thing that we've learned living here is that we may all speak English but we're sure as hell not Anglos. No matter what Bourassa or Parizeau or any of them say, we are Québécois! And we each feel out of place in Canada, in our own way.

I miss Montreal. And I want to go home. But can't 'cause I promised my mother I'd give it a year. Three months down, nine to go. Meanwhile, rain rain rain rain rain rain rain.

Write soon. And if you get back to Montreal, tell her I love her.

Your friend,

Lorena

PS. I almost forgot. I met a man.

23

Flashing disco party lights and dance music, LORENA *dances and imagines she is eating food.*

LORENA   (*voice-over*) Steamies at Montreal Pool Room.
Smoked meat at Schwartz's.
Schuller's kosher barbecue potato chips.

Cott's Black Cherry soda, 'cause if it's Cott it's got to be good!
Dry garlic spareribs at the Dragon Inn on Decarie.
Cream cheese party sandwiches from the Snowdon Deli.
Orange tarts at Café Castillo on Sherbrooke by the Cinema V.
Sunday brunch at Les Filles du Roi.
Praline and ice cream crepes at Le Petit Halle.
Hamburgers and French fries at Lafleur's.
The lobster festival at Amazona's on Côte-St.-Luc.
Bagels from the Bagel Factory on Fairmont.
Pineapple chicken at Lung Fung's.
Bar-B-Barn ribs.
A cabane à sucre breakfast with scrambled eggs, baked beans, back
bacon, home fries, and tourtière.
Chicken at the Chalet BBQ.
Onion bhaji's at the Star of India.
Blueberry cheesecake at Le Commençal.

I crave the flavours of my past and long to taste again the city that
I love to eat. I will devour Montreal, savouring each sweet-and-
sour memory that bursts upon my tongue. I will dine at eight, and
until three, I'll gorge myself with reverie and laugh again with
those I loved!

I'm going home. Home. Where the heart is. Where the hate is.
Where the have to, hard to, happy to is. The prodigal daughter
returns with a hunger.

(*voice-over*) Chocolate cake at Friday's.
Pendeli's Pizza.
Coquilles St. Jacques and profiteroles at Chez Delmos on Notre
Dame.
Three-fish terrine at La Rapiere.
Hot polish sausage at the Café Prague.

    Slide—triplex house at 6180 Durocher.

6180 Durocher still stands.
And though the filmy white curtains
have been many times replaced
with those of other styles,
by those of other tastes,
the long glass door panels
still gleam
invitingly.
I dare not ring the bell
and ask to mount those steps
again.
I've crossed that threshold many times.

Let other lives
play out their mundane dramas
between those walls.
I am content
to stand outside
imagining
the secret and familiar spaces
I once knew
to be mine.

> *Slide—Schwartz's restaurant.*

Schwartz's is still packed
and spicy smelling!
Pickled peppers
medium fat
double mustard
greasy fingers
slipping
on the cold tin
of my black cherry pop.

> *Slide—Chalet BBQ.*

And lunch at Chalet BBQ
is still the cheapest deal in town.
But Café Prague... gone.

> *Slide—the images come up empty, just white light. Repeated throughout the scene.*

Dragon Inn—gone.

> *Slide—empty.*

Star of India—gone.

> *Slide—empty.*

Café Castillo—gone.

> *Slide—empty.*

Le Petite Halle—gone.

> *Slide—empty.*

Lung Fung's—gone.

> *Slide—empty.*

Finast's—gone.

> *Slide—empty.*

Frank's—gone.

Slide—empty.

Strathcona Academy—gone.

Slide—empty.

Guy-Drummond—gone.

Slide—empty.

Each pilgrimage finds that Mecca's disappeared without a
forwarding address.

Slide—store window with "à louer" and "à vendre" signs.

St. Catherine Street feels empty.
The hollow-eyed store windows,
once dazzling with bargains,
stare blankly behind
À louer and
À vendre
signs.

Slide—Peel and St. Catherine streets.

I stand
on the corner of Peel and St. Catherine,
at five P.M. on Thursday,
waiting for the light to change,
feeling cramped
by the buildings
that I'm seeing for the first time
without
their payday crowds.
I cross the street
alone.

Slide—Grumpy's Bar.

I delight at finding
Grumpy's
still downstairs
But my once nightly retreat
no longer feels jazzy
nor exclusive
with its pub style
renovations
and my booze buddies have all
moved on
in body and in spirit
or aged
beyond my recognition.

I drink a toast
to the last echoing
"last call" laughter'
of my past
and leave
drunk
with disapointment.

Montreal and I have changed.
She does not bear
the weight of
her depression well.
But sags
like baggy stockings
around
an old woman's ankles.
And I have become accustomed to
green
West-coast surroundings.
"Go to the farthest place
and work your way back…
if you have to.
You can always come home…
if you have to,"
my mother said.
But even she is gone.

24

Slide—interior of Joe's Café.

LORENA   (*speaking directly to the audience*) And this is what I was going to tell my friend before I was so rudely interrupted. I had gone to Montreal to visit my mother's grave. It had been three heartbroken years since she died. I needed, not only to make my peace with her, but to make sure that she'd been buried in the right spot.

You see, my mother never liked the heat. And some graves are right out there in the open. I didn't want her sweating in the sun for all eternity. So I specifically requested a shady plot beneath the tree. But she died in January. The tree was naked and spindly. And I guess the ground was too frozen to turn because when I left the cemetery her casket was still sitting out on one of those portable folding tables on the spot designated for her burial. The ground hadn't even been broke. For all I knew she was still sitting out there.

I needed the closure of seeing that she had been committed to the ground.

Now, my mother was buried in Memorial Park Cemetery in Ville St-Laurent. My friend Andrew offered to drive me. And though I had the vague recollection of the cemetery being on Côte-de-Liesse, just past the National Film Board, I thought to check the address before we left.

So I look in the White Pages and it's not there. I look in the Yellow Pages and it's not there either. I think, okay. You're in Quebec now. Translate. I look under Parc Memorial. Nothing. Cemetaire Memorial. Nada. I call the information operator and she insists that there is no such listing.

Now I am really in a panic. A whole fucking cemetery can't just get up and walk away. Where the hell is my mother!?

We hop in the car, drive up Cremazie, onto the Metropolitan, exit on Côte-de-Liesse… and bam! The one-eyed guy and the NFB are right where I remember 'em. We drive a little further and come to the high stone walls of the cemetery. It too is right where I remember it.

I'm thinking, "Now, what the hell just happened there?" Maybe the cemetery just got filled up and stopped advertising. We'll drive up to the gates and see a red neon sign flashing "No Vacancy" or "Standing Room Only."

We see a sign all right and it is not amusing. It says, "Les Jardins Urgel Bourgie."

Les Jardins Urgel Bourgie! That's no translation for Memorial Park! Les Jardins Urgel Bourgie! It's an Urgel Bourgie cemetery! They sold the fucking cemetery to Urgel Bourgie!

Urgel Bourgie is a large French undertaking company. My mother hated them! She always said, "I've had to live my life in French. I want to die in English. Stick me in an English cemetery like Memorial Park. And no matter how cheap it is, don't let those Urgel Bourgie people touch me." And now she's decomposing in the shadow of their sign. I hear her cursing in her grave.

They could have, at least, informed me of their intent to sell. I would like to have had the chance to voice my opinion on their decision. Or at least given my consent. But this was decided independently of me, like so many decisions being made in and around Quebec.

I found my mother right where I had left her. Only six feet under. And it was as I requested—a shady spot beneath a spreading maple tree. I sat a moment and contemplated her epitaph: "Too well loved to be forgotten." I noticed at least a half a dozen other grave stones in her immediate vicinity that bore the same inscription. There must have been a sale that year. "Too well loved to be forgotten." Aw, Ma. How could I ever forget?

Whiteout.

25

Footlights come up, projecting LORENA's *shadow on the screen.*

LORENA

Je retrouve l'espoir. Et soudanement, ma lueur est là, en face de moi.

Et je trouve que ce point à l'horizon blanc n'est pas une roche ni un tronc d'arbre. Mais une femme, noire et toute nue dans la neige. Je ne peux pas voir son visage—son dos est tourné ver moi. Mais je sais qu'elle n'était pas aveuglé par les rayon do soleil ni gené le froid.

Elle ce tient toute droite sa tête—haute et fière. Ses mains—placé hautenement sure les hances—et les pieds plantées solidement sure terre.

Elle a l'air complètement chez elle, indifférent à cet environnement hostile.

Qui est cette femme qui défie les elements et ose revendiquer cet endroit pour elle-même?

Je s'approche lentement et pose la main sur son épaule. Ma main tremble. J'ai peur. Elle s'est tourné vers moi et je réalise alors qu'elle est moi.

C'est moi!

Et je me réveille.

Blackout.

26

Lights come up. LORENA *places the chair back in its original position. Music is playing:* LORENA *singing "Une Québécoise errante" (recorded).*

LORENA

On October 30, 1995, I felt as if I'd come dangerously close to being severed from both my personal and family histories. And Parizeau's remarks regarding "pûr laine" and "ethnics" made it clear that the years and generations my family has invested in

Québec were perceived to be of no consequence or value. We would never be accepted as Québécois. Because we are Black and English-speaking, we did not have the right to love Quebec, to speak to that love, or to vote for it.

When I moved to Canada, I did not stop being a Québécoise. I discovered that I had always been one. I did not forfeit my identity. I gained it.

I am expatriate anglophone, Montréalaise, Québécoise. These are just a few of the memories of a life I lived in the land of my birth. I cannot be separated from them. They cannot be legislated out of being. Nor can the Supreme Court rule on their validity. They are a part of the distinct whole that is me.

Memory serves me.
An exile
in Canada.

Blackout.

The End.

Born in Montreal, **Lorena Gale** was an award-winning actress, director, and writer who worked extensively in theatres across Canada. Her first play, *Angelique*, was the winner of the duMaurier National Playwriting Competition and was nominated Outstanding New Play in Calgary's Betty Mitchell Awards. Her solo performance, *Je me souviens: memories of an expatriate Anglophone, Montréalaise, Québécoise exiled in Canada*, premiered in Eastern Front Theatre's On the Waterfront Festival in Halifax and was produced at One Yellow Rabbit's High Performance Rodeo in Calgary, the Firehall Theatre in Vancouver, and the Belfry Theatre in Victoria. Lorena passed away in 2009.